ONELINERS

How the Line Speaks to Your Mind

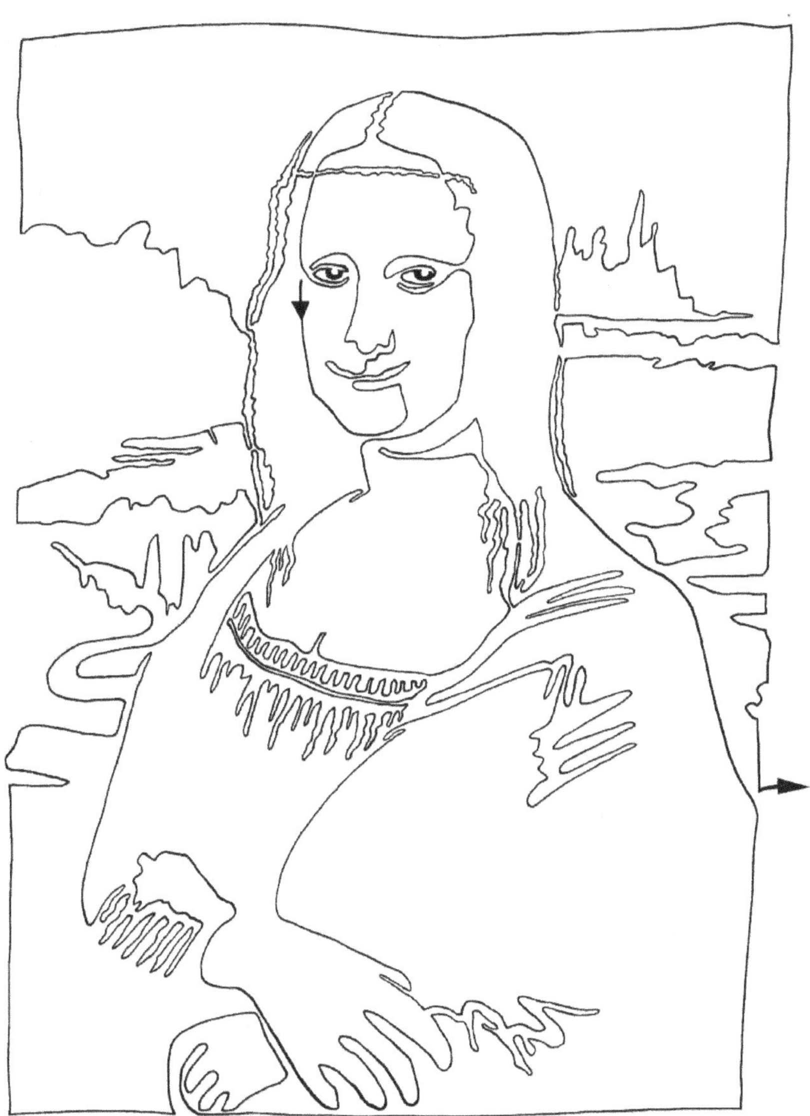

Getting a Line on Mona Lisa

ONELINERS

How the Line Speaks to Your Mind

Written and Illustrated
By Richard O. Calkins

Published by

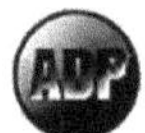

A Different Perception

First edition

Library of Congress Catalog Card Number: 2013907625

ISBN: 978-0-9836770-2-4

To my wife Beth and my daughters Trina and Teresa.
May you always have the same joy in your lives
as you have brought into mine.

Other Books by Richard O. Calkins

Relativity Revisited

Adages and Aphorisms from Philosophilus

The Problem With Relativity

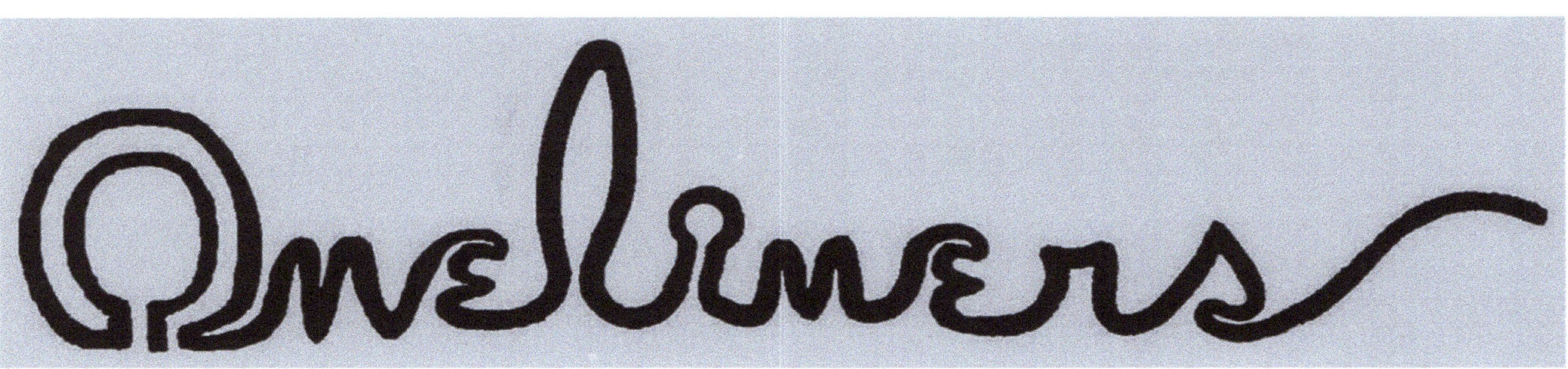

Table of Contents

You are about to become a magician by learning how to conjure and control the power of the line. Understanding how the line communicates with your subconscious will enhance your ability to understand and appreciate works of art. It also will empower you to communicate your own perceptions and emotions.

Young people will love this book for its humor, novelty, and unique Oneliner illustrations. But its role for adults is very serious: education and empowerment. This book uses humor as a teaching tool. It helps you learn by making the experience more enjoyable; and people tend to remember things that make them laugh. But the objective of Oneliners is to show, clearly and conclusively, how a line uses psychology to communicate. That's serious business and has a significant payoff.

A line exercises power by making us see things that aren't really there and by selectively stimulating our thoughts and emotions. It's all in how the line is drawn. In this fun and easy to read book, you'll learn how the line identifies objects and communicates their characteristics; and, for animate objects, how the line communicates such things as their attitudes, actions, and emotions. You will learn how a single unbroken line can tell a story. You will even learn how the entire universe could be captured on a single unbroken line. The power of the line is truly immense for those who understand it.

Nearly every art instruction book tells us that drawing is the foundation of art. This includes the activity of arranging shapes and colors that we call painting. The reason is that using lines to discover the specific characteristics which will best communicate what we want to say shows us how to organize a painting that will deliver our message.

It is unfortunate that many painters dislike drawing and studiously avoid it, believing that playing with lines has little to do with arranging shapes and colors. It is equally unfortunate that many beginning artists are discouraged by expectations of failure because they "can't even draw a straight line." This book intends to dispel both myths so that accomplished artists will gladly take up line work to create even better compositions and fledgling artists will know that not drawing straight lines can be a blessing, not a curse.

Chapter 1
What Are Oneliners?

To demonstrate the power of the line as clearly and as forcefully as possible, every drawing, every object, and every example in this book is drawn with a single uninterrupted line. That line does not cross itself nor even touch itself from its beginning to its end, hence the term Oneliners. By limiting every illustration to a single uninterrupted line you can be absolutely certain that everything you see, everything you feel, and everything you think about it is caused by the characteristics of that single line as it wanders across the paper. That one line is the only thing that's there. For the same reason, it was necessary to restrict the illustrations to black and white; otherwise there might be an unrecognized response to color, which would introduce unwanted ambiguities. The purity of this approach and the challenge of producing complex illustrations using a single unbroken line make this book unique.

Types of Oneliners

There are basically three types of Oneliners: constrained, open, and closed. Constrained Oneliners are the least useful of the bunch, so let's get a definition out of the way and then concentrate on the other two.

Constrained Oneliners

Constrained Oneliners have at least one end buried inside where you can't get at it to connect to another Oneliner. It's forever isolated from inclusion in a larger context, except perhaps at the very beginning or end of the line. That doesn't mean that they have no value. Many things can be expressed well by a constrained Oneliner, but they can't be chained with other Oneliners into a continuum. In that sense they are constrained.

The only constrained Oneliner in this book is the cover drawing of the Mona Lisa. The best way to draw it without doing violence to the serenity and symmetry of her face was to start next to her eye in the interior of the drawing and work outward. Perhaps that's just another demonstration of the exquisite mystery that is Mona Lisa.

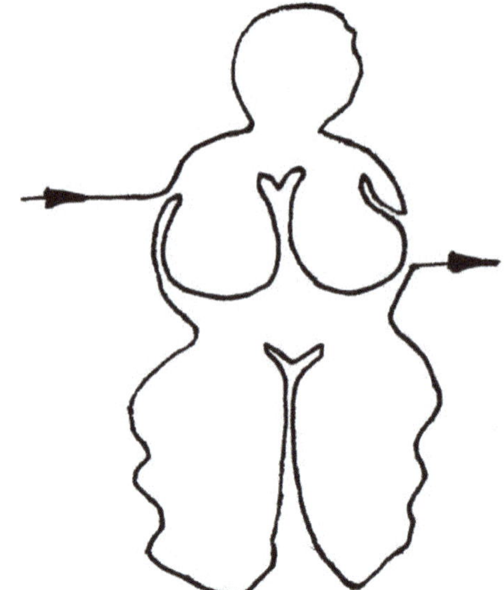

An open Oneliner has a visible beginning and a separate visible end, both of which are readily accessible to connect to other Oneliners. Between its beginning and end the line can go wherever it wants as long as it doesn't cross or touch itself along the way. Throughout this book, arrows are shown at the beginning and end of open Oneliners to make them clearly visible.

Open Oneliner
Prehistoric fertility figurine

Closed Oneliners

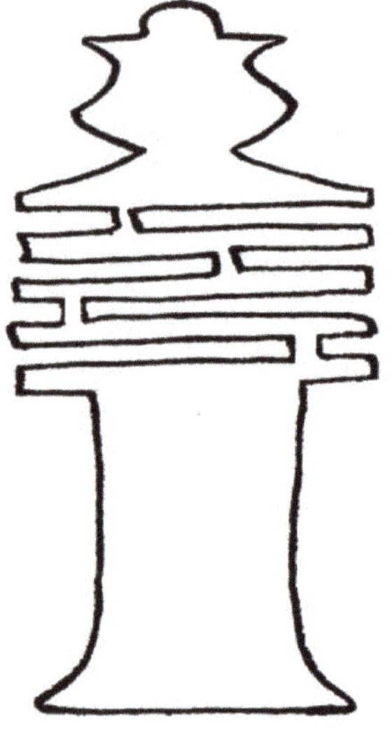

A closed Oneliner has no visible beginning or end. However complex its path, it forms a closed loop. You can start following it at any point and will eventually end up back at that point without the line having crossed or touched itself along the way.

Closed Oneliner
Ancient Egyptian Djed Pillar

Open Oneliners can be chained indefinitely by connecting the end of one to the beginning of another, leading to ever increasing complexity. The chain can be left open or it can be closed by connecting the exit of the last link to the entrance of the first. Of course, once you do that, the distinction between last and first becomes inoperative and it becomes a closed Oneliner.

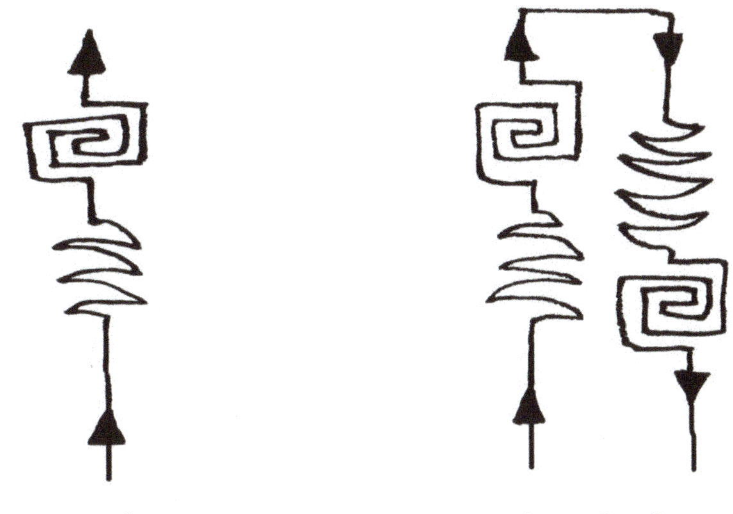

Open Oneliner

Open Oneliner
Created by chaining two
shorter Oneliners

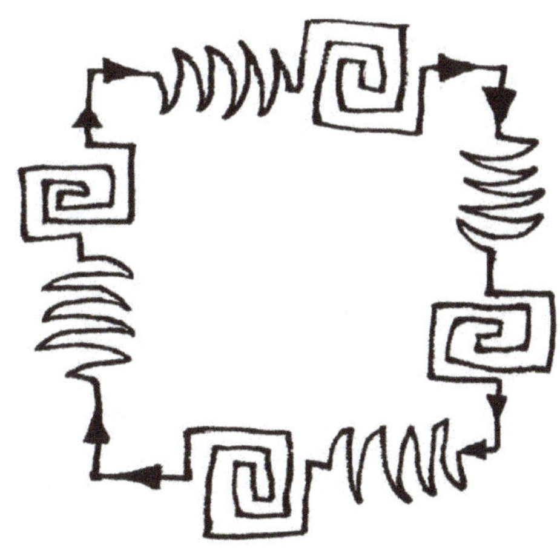

Closed Oneliner
Created by chaining four shorter Oneliners.
Arrows are shown to identify the shorter
Oneliners used in the chain.

A closed Oneliner can be opened nearly anywhere on its perimeter by breaking the line and adding an entry and exit. Essentially that converts it into an open Oneliner. This allows us either to connect it to another Oneliner or to insert it seamlessly inside another Oneliner. For example, this closed Oneliner of an automobile is not devoid of interest but does look a bit static. Interest can be added by putting it into a larger context. This can be done by breaking it in the right places to insert it into another Oneliner.

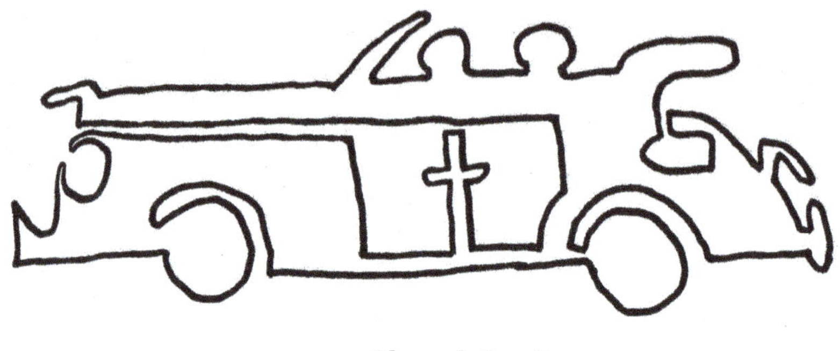

Closed Oneliner
Automobile

This desert scene looks barren and almost lifeless, but by inserting the automobile, it could be more interesting too.

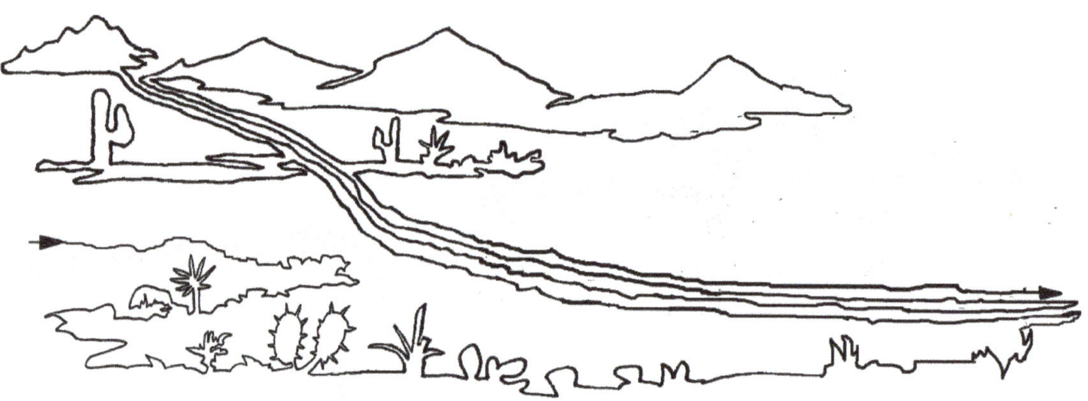

Open Oneliner
Desert Scene

In this drawing the previously closed Oneliner automobile has been opened in two separate places to integrate it into the landscape. One opening is on the front bumper and the other is at the bottom of the front tire. The desert scene has been modified to make space in the road for the car and to add the dust cloud behind it. The end result is still a single unbroken line that neither crosses itself nor touches itself from beginning to end. What you now see and how it makes you feel is a result of the characteristics and path of that single line.

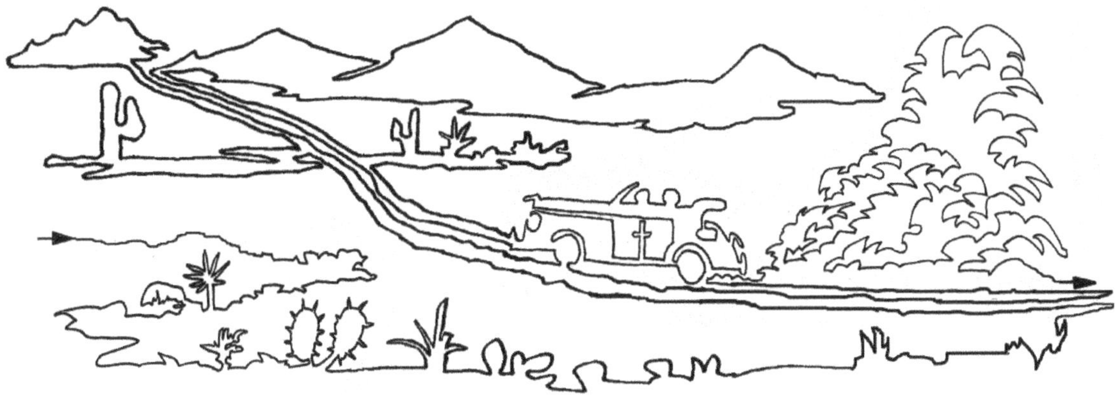

Open Oneliner
Automobile Racing across a Desert

That relatively sparse line tells a story about people in an open convertible racing down an unimproved dirt road across a flat expanse of desert toward something in the distance by a range of low barren mountains. Who are they? Where are they going? Why are they in such a hurry? The rearrangement of the line to incorporate both the automobile and the landscape captures our interest and provokes our curiosity. Yet what actually is there is a single uninterrupted line wandering around on a piece of paper.

Chapter 2
The Sources of a Line's Power

To be able to conjure and control the power of the line, we need to understand where that power comes from and how it works. There are two fundamental sources of the power of the line. The first is that a line can evoke the appearance of objects that are endowed with emotional content. The second is that we respond emotionally to the characteristics of the line itself. If we put the two together in a mutually supportive way their effects are multiplied. To clearly understand how this works, let's first look at some examples of how objects we see can affect how we feel. Next, we'll examine how we respond to different line characteristics. Then we'll see how the two sources of power can be put together in a mutually supportive way.

Objects Have Innate Emotional Content

Objects have innate emotional content in the human psyche both because of instincts stored away in our DNA and because of the human experiences we all have in common that are stored in our memories. Here are some examples of objects that have emotional content.

Kittens always make us feel warm and mushy. So do little chicks. A kitty surrounded by admiring chicks could be a sugar overload.

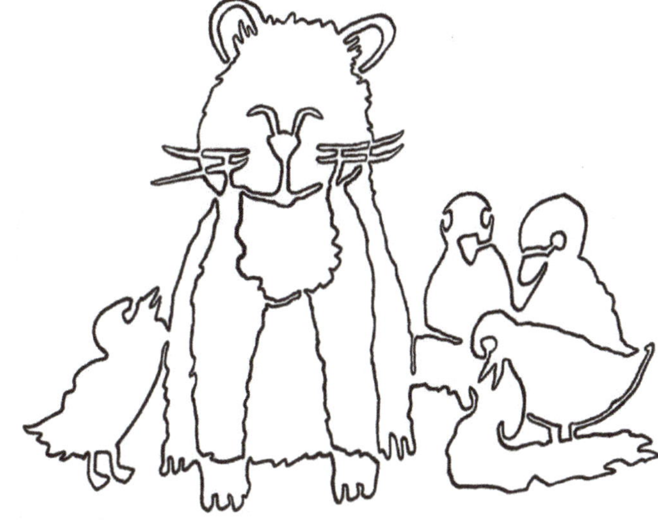

Man's best friend! He's not only lovable, he can be funny too. Thinking about a happy-go-lucky mutt scratching an itch makes us smile.

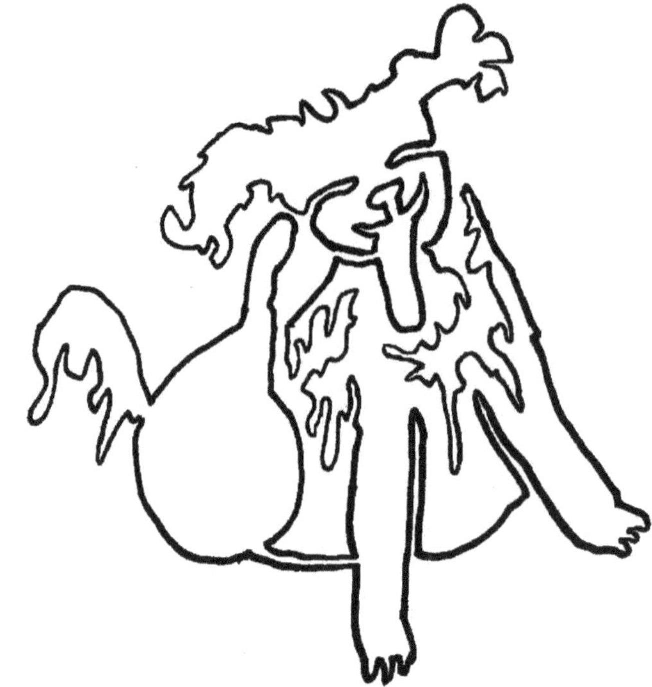

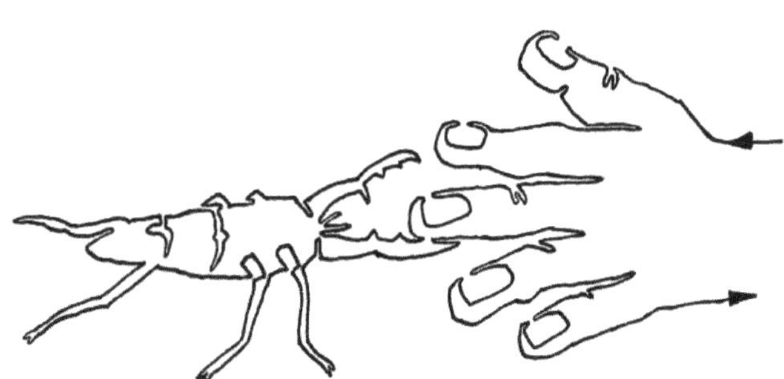

There aren't many things that can make us as queasy as a big bug, especially if he is about to take a sample of someone's finger.

However, a spider can make us even more uncomfortable than a bug, particularly if it's large, hairy, and looking right at us. How would you like to pick it up and hold it in your hand? I'm told that they can be quite friendly.

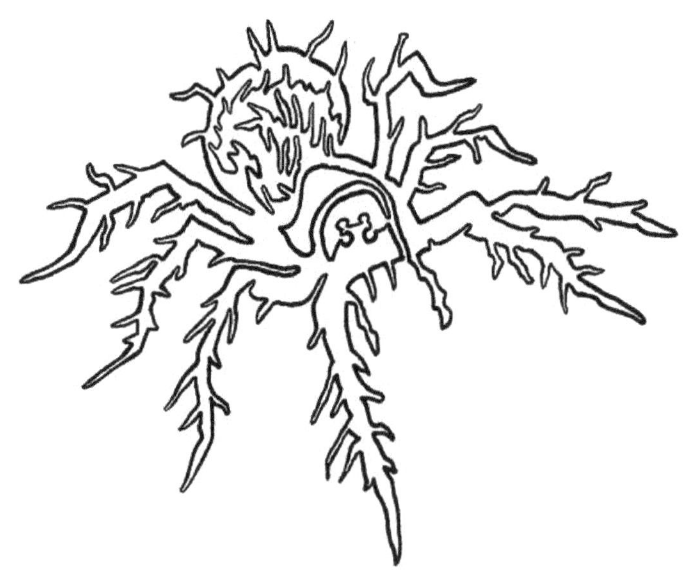

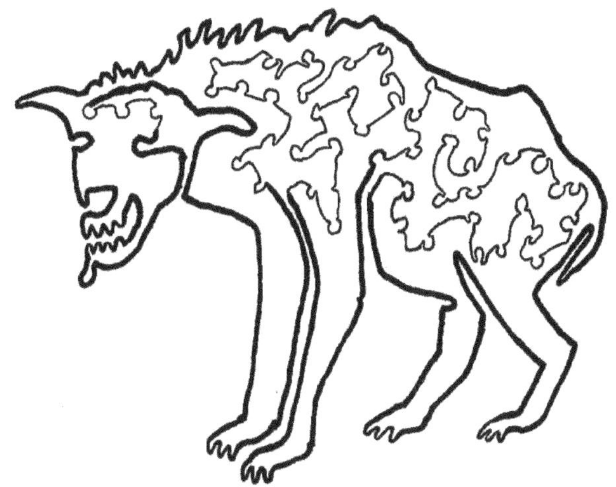

Isn't it interesting that we can feel all warm and fuzzy about a happy-go-lucky mutt but not feel at all the same way about a hyena? They both have very similar body structure. It must be the hyena's grace and loving demeanor that make the difference. NOT!

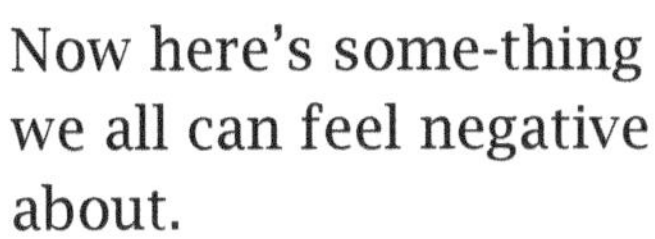

Now here's some-thing we all can feel negative about.

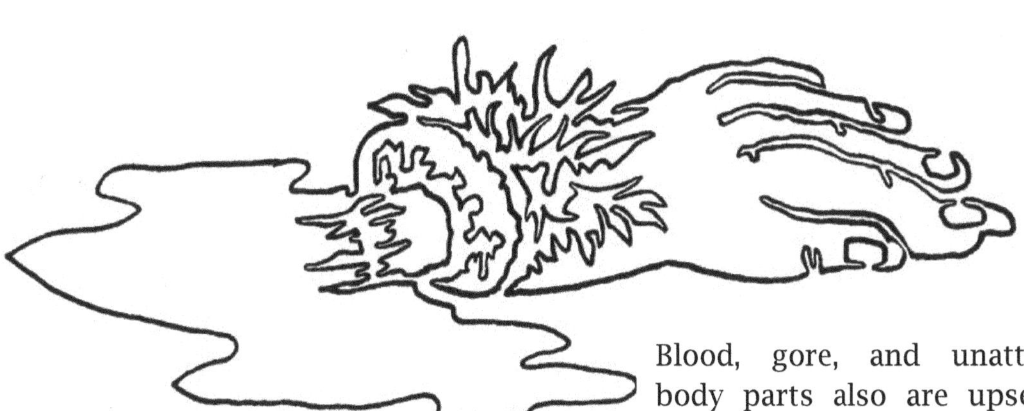

Blood, gore, and unattached body parts also are upsetting, especially if they are really hairy.

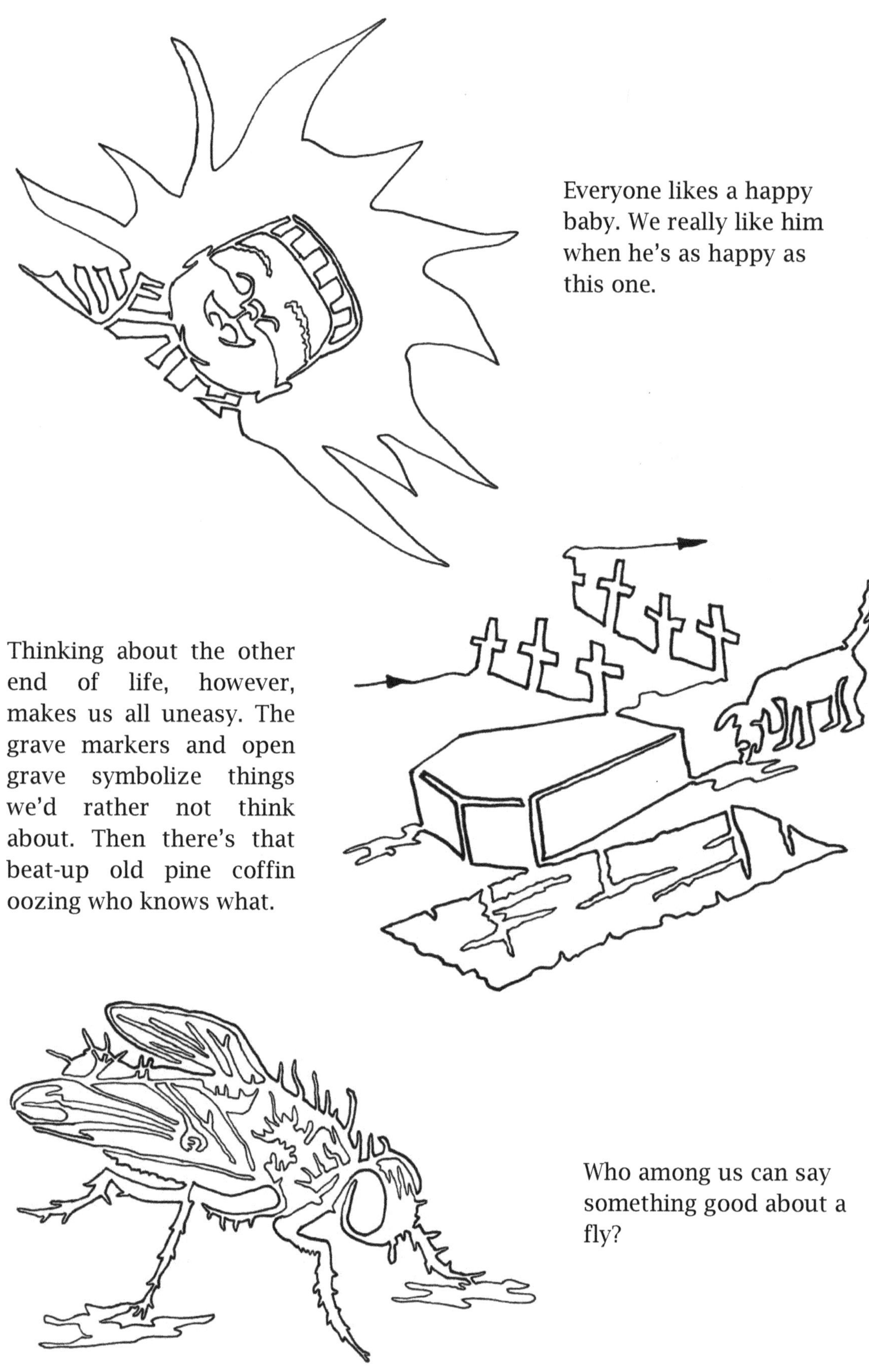

Everyone likes a happy baby. We really like him when he's as happy as this one.

Thinking about the other end of life, however, makes us all uneasy. The grave markers and open grave symbolize things we'd rather not think about. Then there's that beat-up old pine coffin oozing who knows what.

Who among us can say something good about a fly?

I don't think we are going to feel warm and fuzzy about this guy either. Look at those teeth! He's not in a very friendly mood.

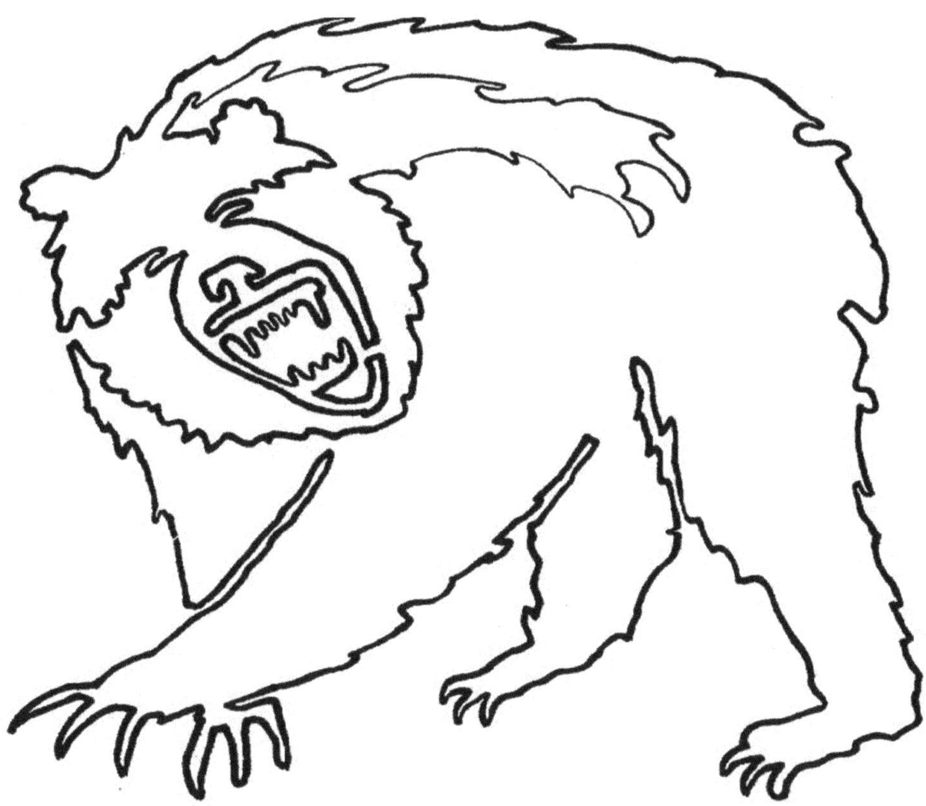

While Mr. Grizzly looks pretty threatening, he's not nearly as scary as if he were right in our face.

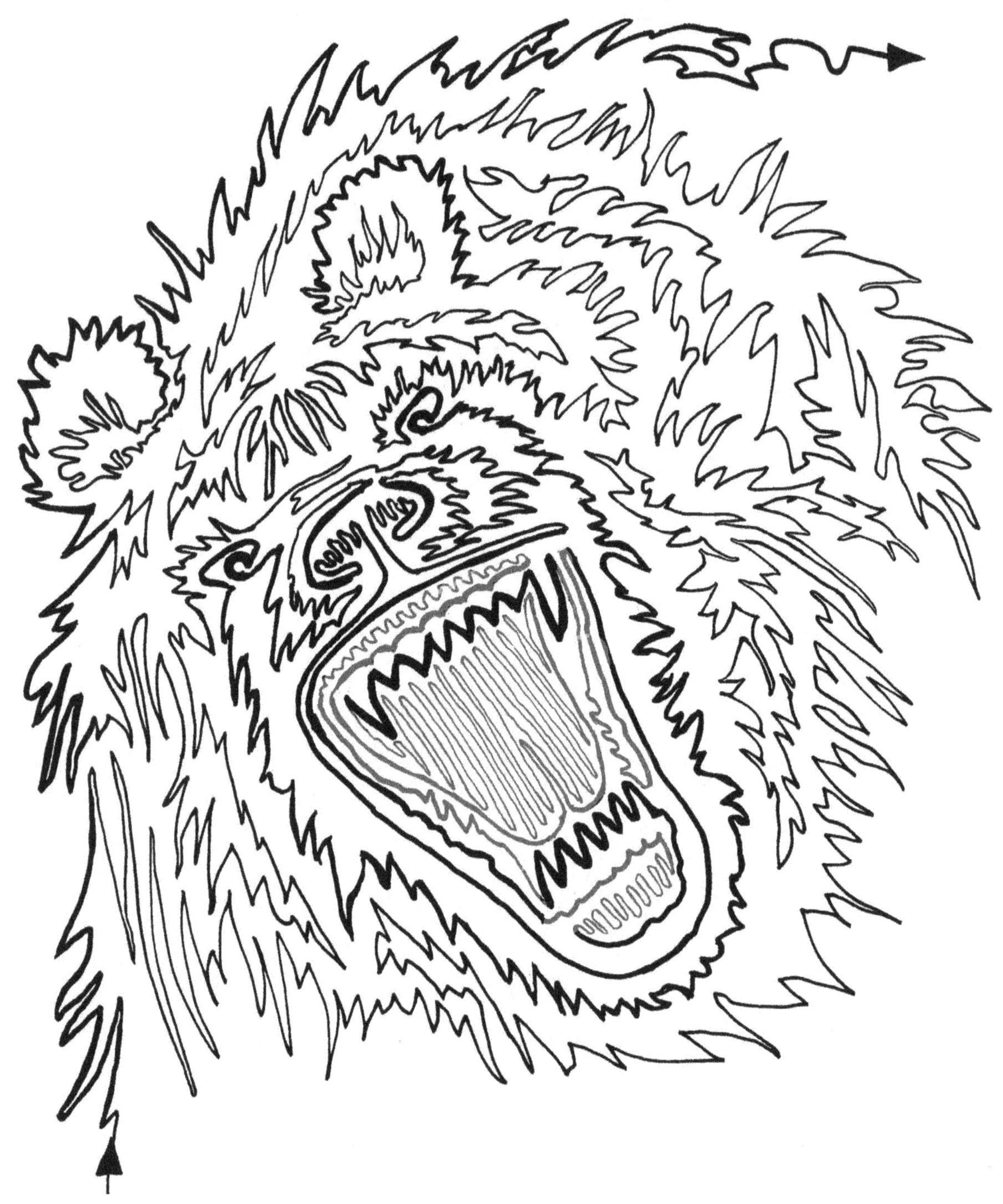

See what I mean?

A thick line is more powerful, more commanding, and more important than a thin line. A thin line can deliver information but it doesn't demand your attention.

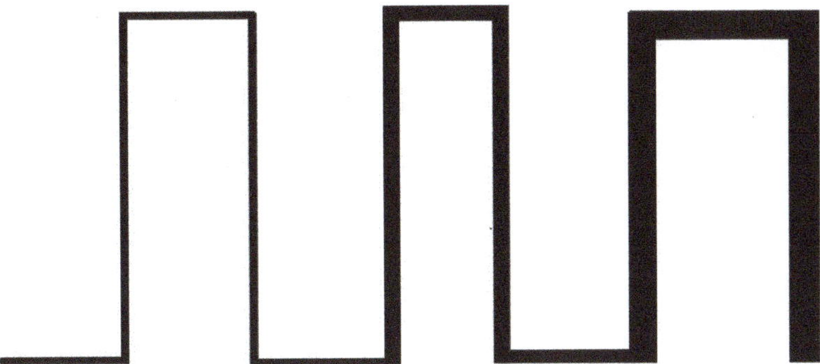

A light line has less importance than a dark line. The darker the line, the more it demands your attention.

For example, most of the lines in the bear's mouth on the previous page were made both thinner and lighter to put more emphasis on the bear's teeth.

A vertical line is serious, proud, strong, upright, and unbending. It commands respect. It can even be a bit intimidating.

A horizontal line is unthreatening. less in your face, more restful, unprepossessing, even inactive.

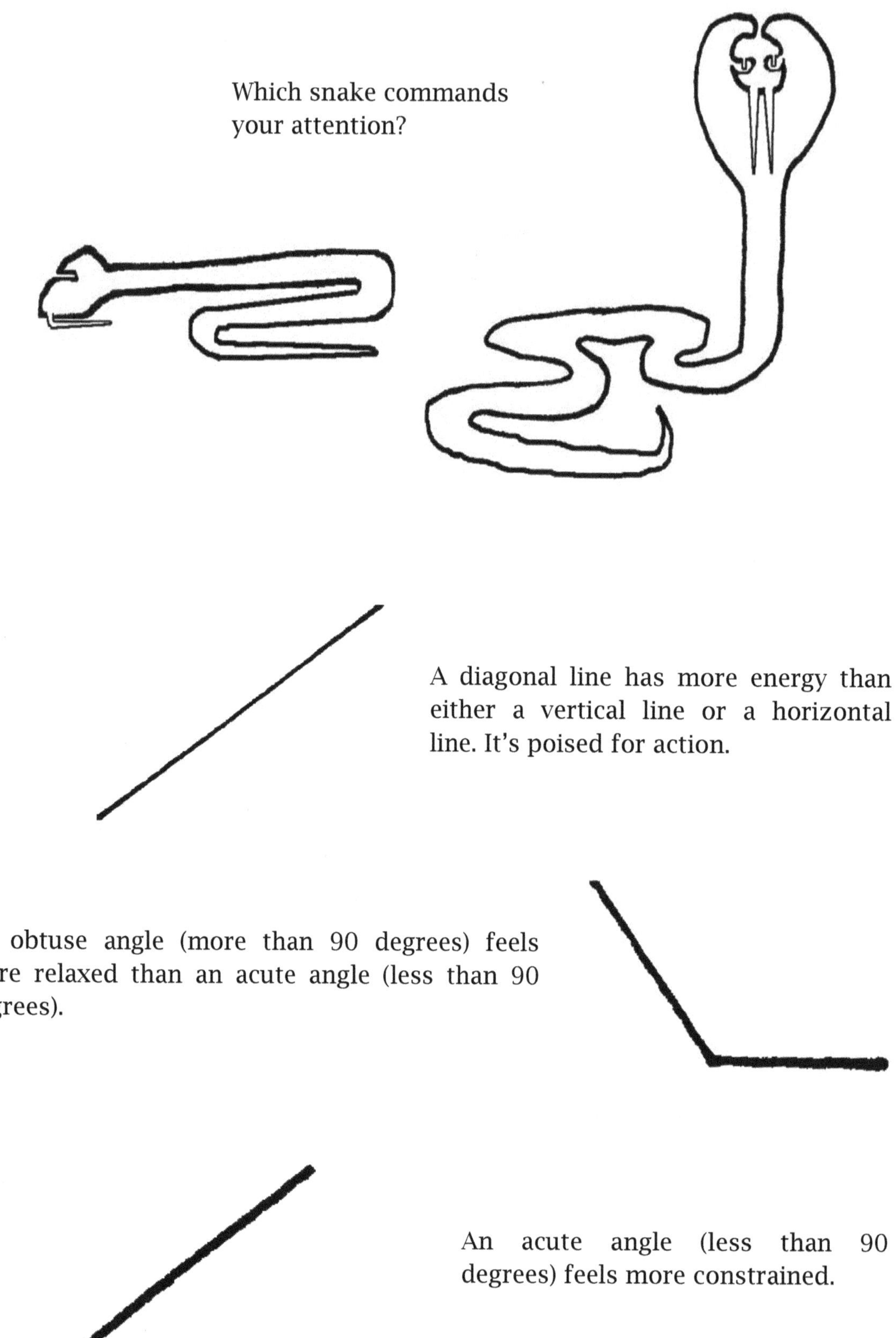

A diagonal line has more energy than either a vertical line or a horizontal line. It's poised for action.

An obtuse angle (more than 90 degrees) feels more relaxed than an acute angle (less than 90 degrees).

An acute angle (less than 90 degrees) feels more constrained.

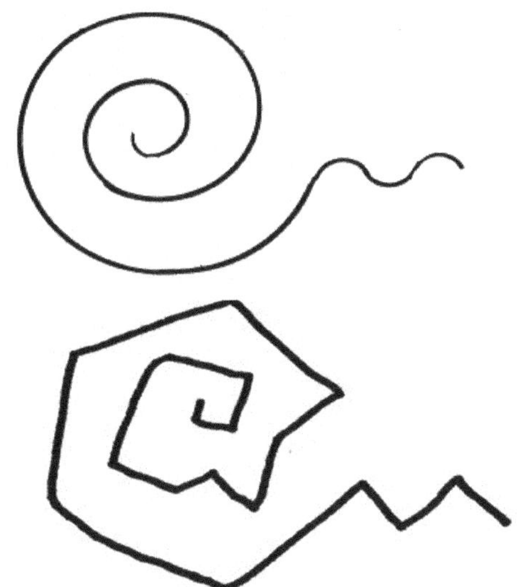

A line with gentle curves is calmer and more relaxing than a line with abrupt changes of direction.

A line with short choppy segments, numerous abrupt corners, close parallel line segments, and boring repetition feels busy, disorganized, claustrophobic, and excessively structured. It is certainly not relaxing.

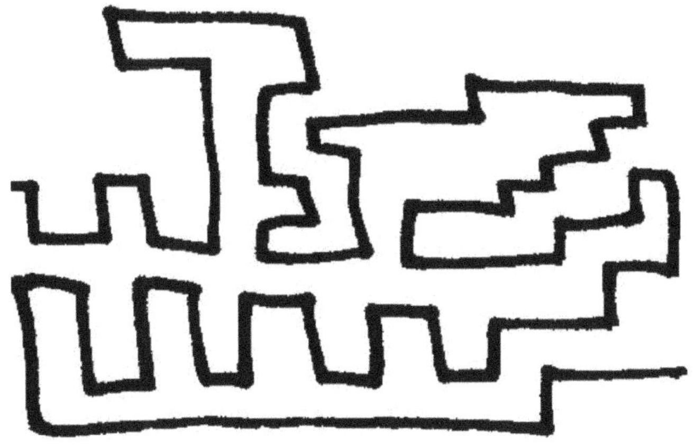

A zigzag line with sharp corners projects energy, action, exuberance, forcefulness. (Go back and look at the dust cloud behind that speeding car in the desert on page 9 and the aura around the happy baby's head on page 14.)

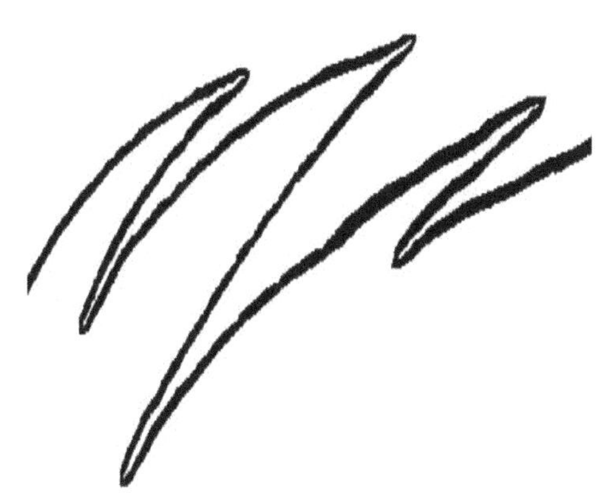

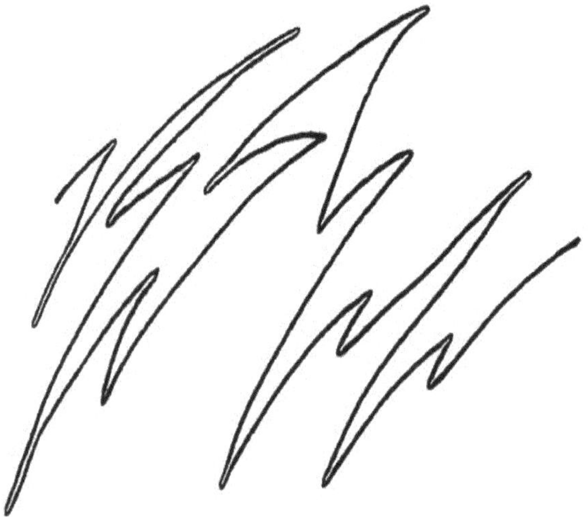

If the zigzags get carried away they can feel unsettling, unpredictable, possibly dangerous - like sharp objects.

Lines that are too simple, too regular, or too repetitive make us feel bored.

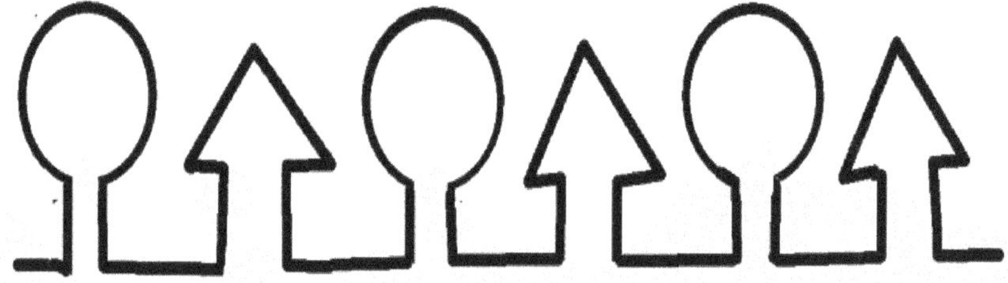

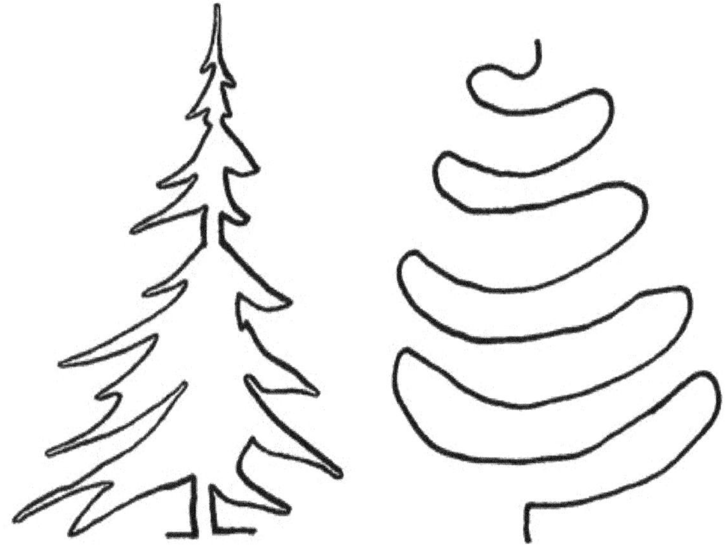

Lines that create a diversity of shape and size are more interesting regardless of whether the subject is objective or abstract.

A group of lines (or line segments) that appear to converge on an imaginary point can give a sense of depth and distance.

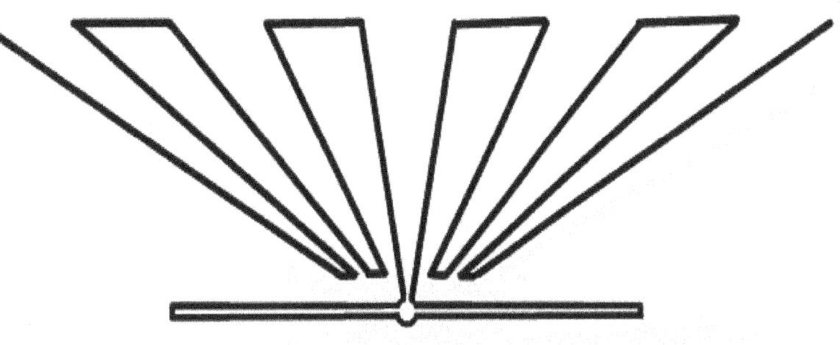

If the imaginary point is below the converging lines, it will appear that we are looking up at them, such as at a ceiling.

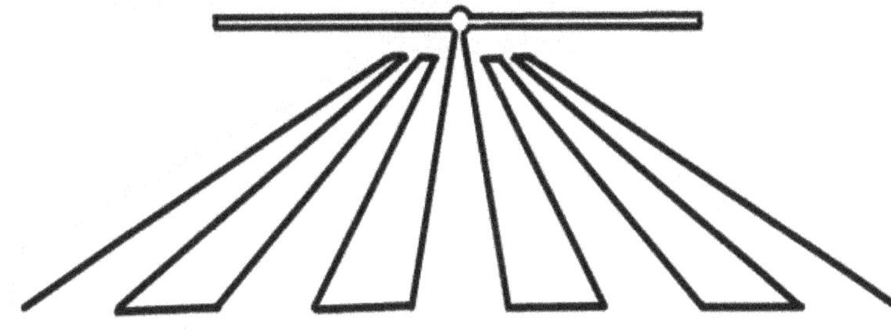

If the imaginary point is above the converging lines, it will appear that we are looking down at them, such as at a field or plain that is below us.

The white horizontal bar captured inside the drawn line represents what is called the horizon line. The white dot on which the line segments converge is called the vanishing point.

If you rotate the converging lines by 90 degrees, they will appear to be on vertical planes that disappear into the distance.

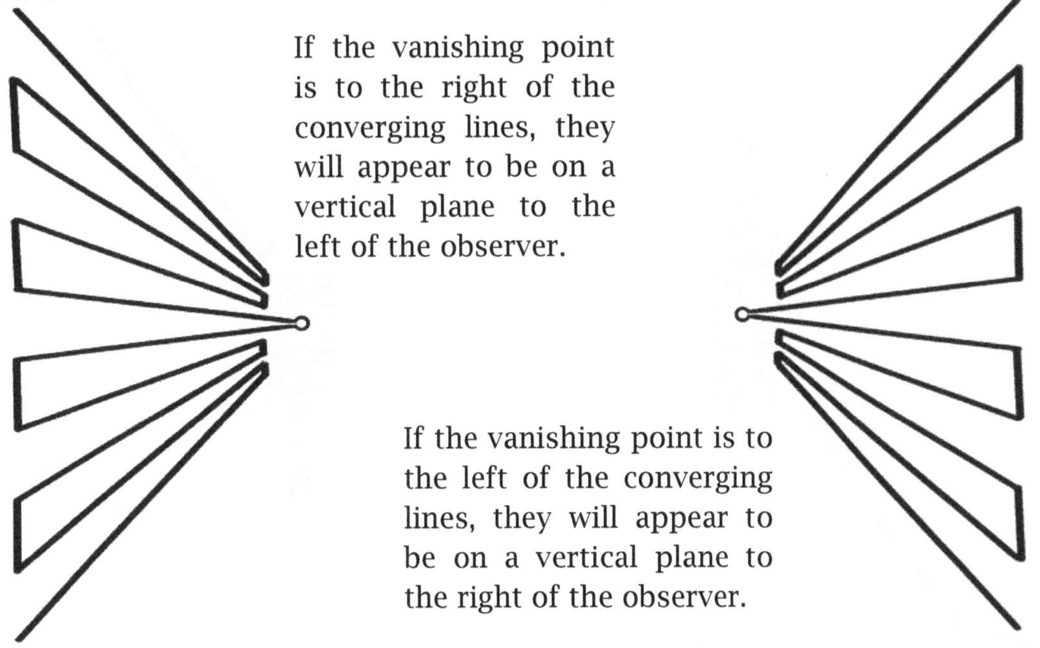

If the vanishing point is to the right of the converging lines, they will appear to be on a vertical plane to the left of the observer.

If the vanishing point is to the left of the converging lines, they will appear to be on a vertical plane to the right of the observer.

It took mankind all of the millennia from when we first scratched stick figures on the walls of caves until the Renaissance to discover this particular power of the line. It is the basis of perspective drawing.

A full description of perspective drawing is a book in itself. However, you can easily teach yourself how it works by drawing some quick sketches that place the imaginary point in various locations, such as above and below the horizon line and to the right and left of the center of the illustration. You have both the power to learn and the power to teach yourself by experimentation. Develop your confidence in that power and use it at your will.

Chapter 3
How to Conjure and Empower Objects

Thus far we have examined the two sources of the power of the line. One is our innate response to the objects the line can cause us to perceive. The other is our response to the characteristics of the line itself. To learn how the power can be conjured most effectively, we will now examine where it exerts its greatest impact: at the silhouette.

Conjuring Identifiable Objects

The key to an object's identity is its silhouette. By itself, it is enough to positively identify almost any object, as in these examples.

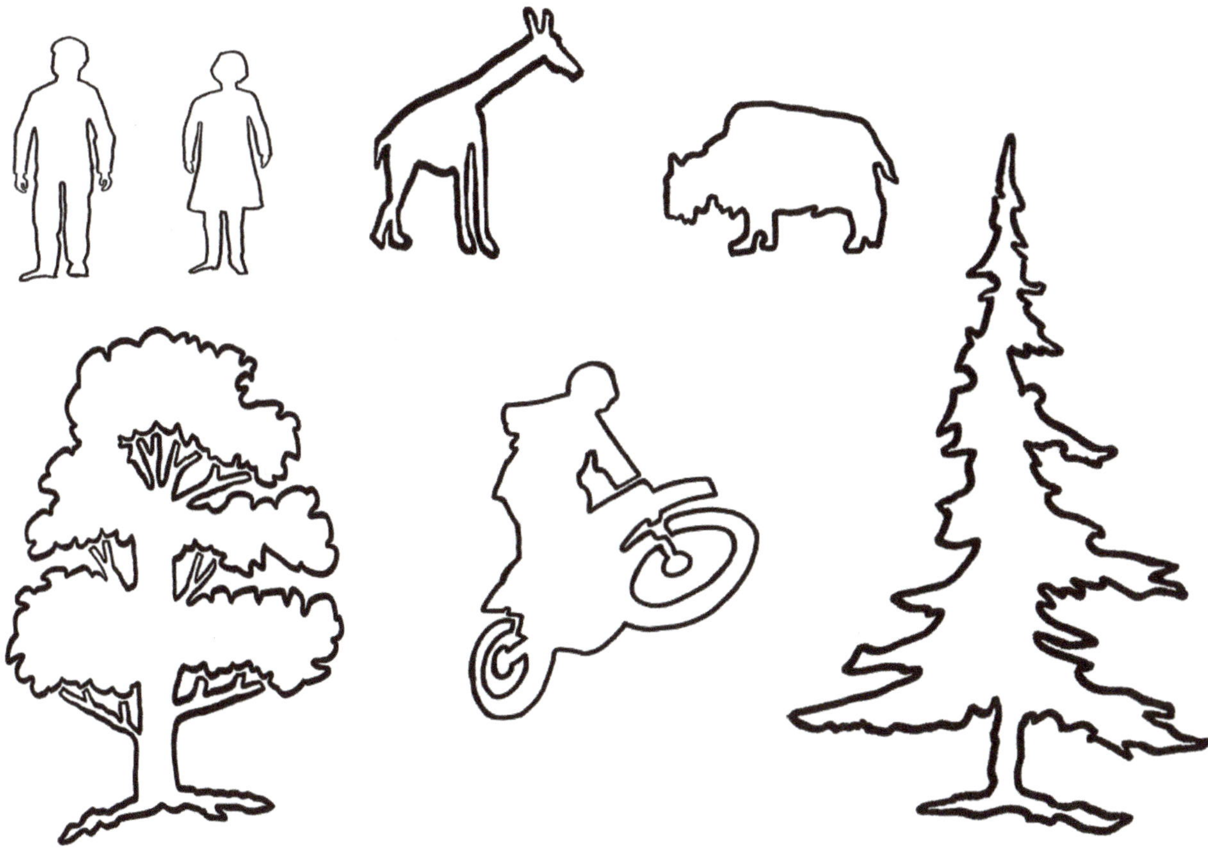

A single silhouette can even be enough to identify a whole group of objects.

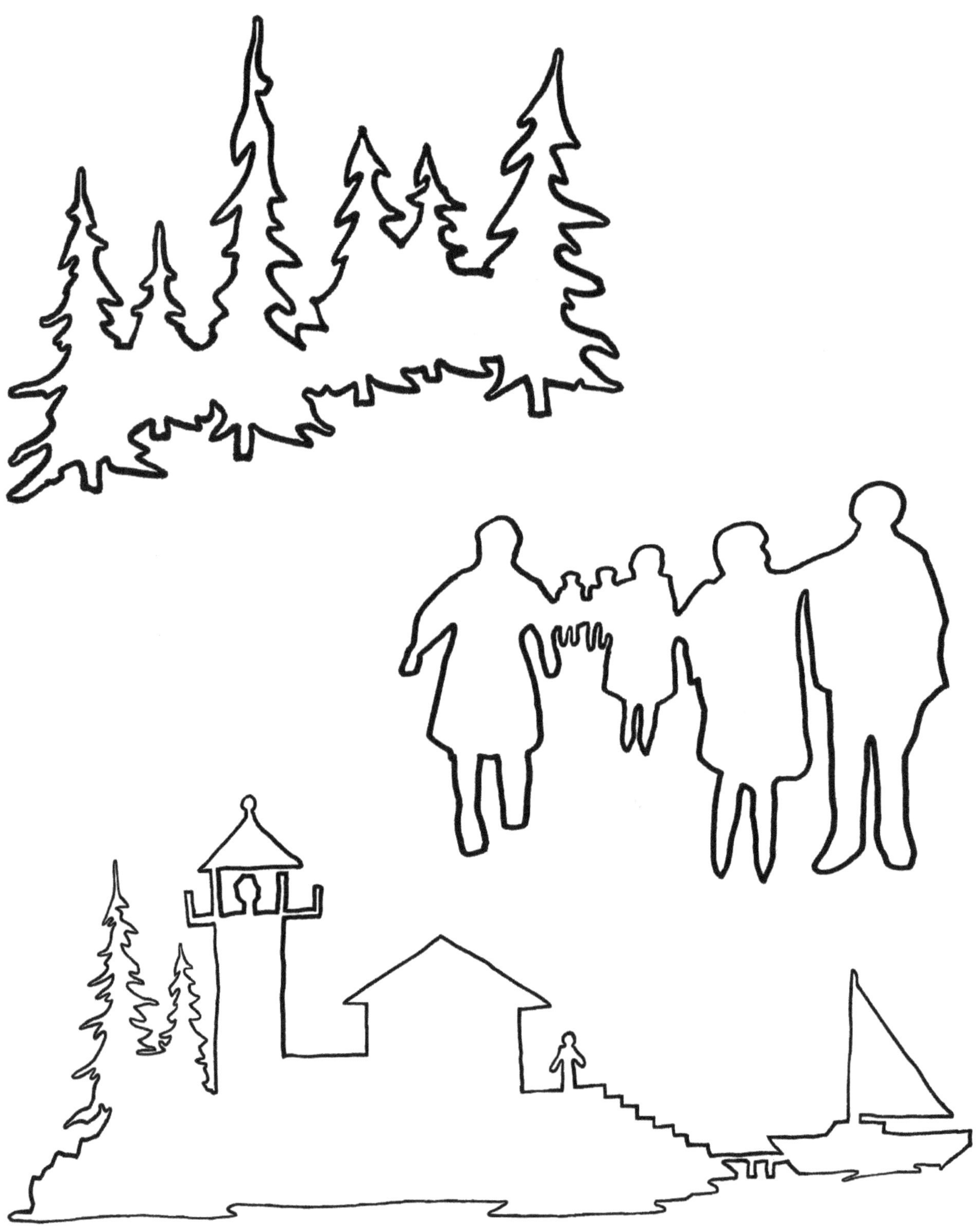

The key to empowering an object lies in the characteristics of the line used to create it. Empowerment means endowing the object with the ability to make us understand its identity and condition and, for an animate object, its actions, emotions, attitude, and intentions. These are what bring our perception of an object to life. Here are some examples of how our perception of a dog changes as the line characteristics of its silhouette change.

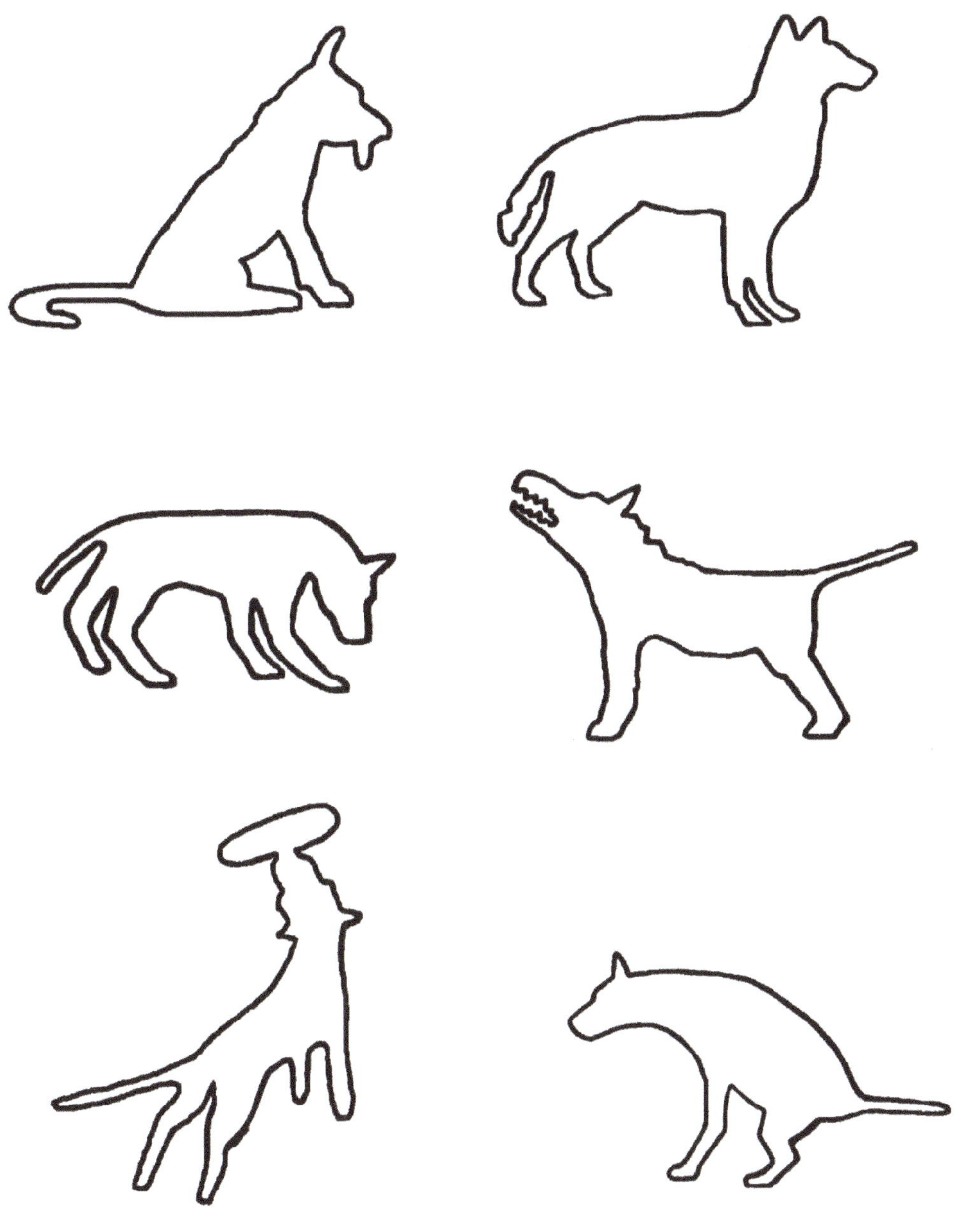

Once you have selected the silhouette and line characteristics to create an empowered object, you can selectively add details to increase its realism and to strengthen your message. It is important, however, to select them purposefully. Anything you add that does not support your message will detract from it.

A good rule of thumb is to limit additions to those that fulfill one of three purposes: reducing ambiguity, adding message-related realism, or providing a message-related environment.

Reducing Ambiguity

Reducing ambiguity is important when the best choice of silhouette is one that doesn't show parts of the object that are important for identification. For example, a horse is most readily identified from a side profile. Suppose, however, that our message is one that requires viewing the horse from the front and slightly above. The silhouette from that point of view will not show the horse's head. When we add the head to the silhouette, the horse is positively identified, reducing ambiguity.

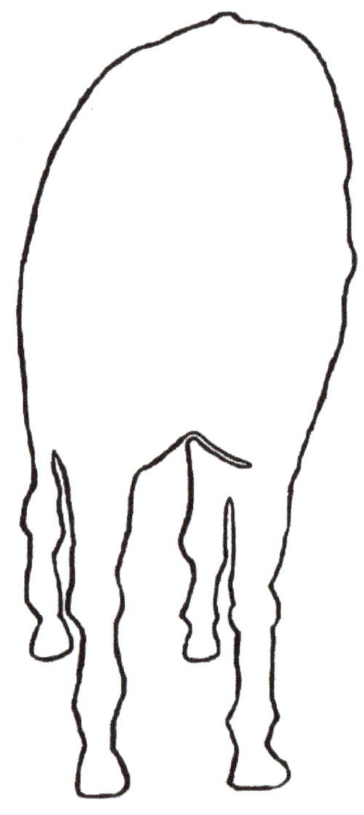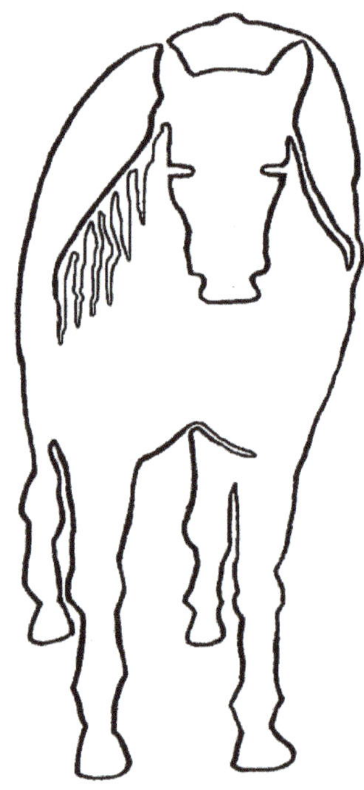

Adding Message-Related Details

The words "message-related" are stated here to emphasize that adding realism does not mean putting in everything you see in your subject material. Adding things simply because they are there is a recipe for delivering a muddle not a message. What you want to do is examine and evaluate everything you add in terms of how characteristic it is of the object and of how it supports your message. Work from the highest priority down. Stop before your drawing starts looking too busy. That last point is a bit more easily said than done but that's where practice and experience come in.

Providing a Message-Related Environment

So far we've dealt with the power of the line as it applies to objects. However, our message about an object or about a group of objects will be enhanced by providing a message-related environment. Suppose we want to say something about someone being mugged in a bad part of town. Our viewer not only will need to see someone who looks like a mugger and one who looks like a muggee, but also some run-down buildings, beat-up old cars, and debris that looks like the bad part of town. Conjuring and empowering each of these requires applying the power of the line.

Applying the Three Purposes Together

For an example of applying the three purposes together, let's use the grizzly bear that threatened earlier. The most easily identifiable silhouette for a grizzly bear is a side view. However the message of being threatened requires him to be looking at us. This position puts his head inside the silhouette of his body, which introduces ambiguity.

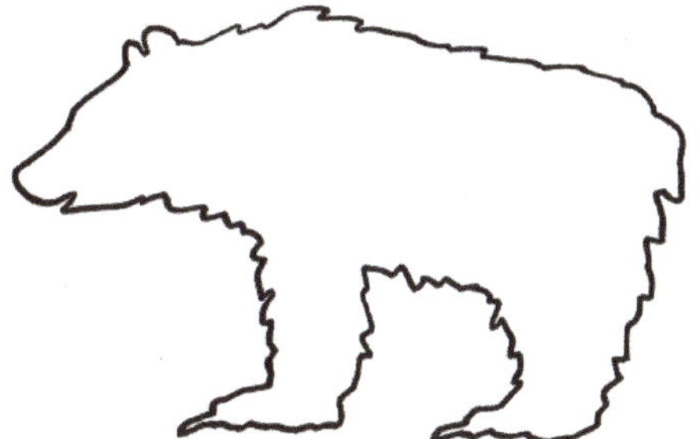 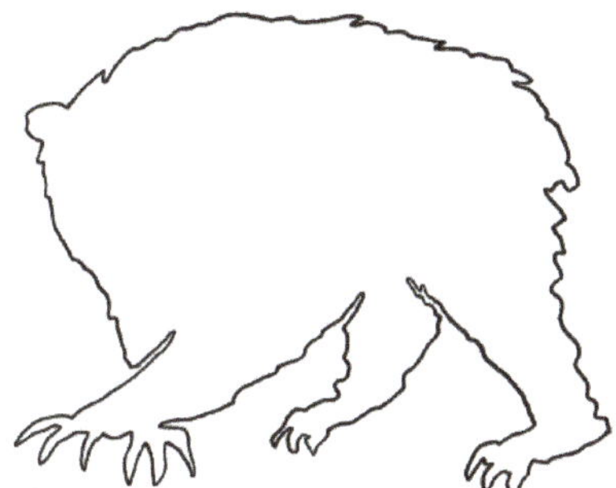

To reduce that ambiguity and add some message-related details, we need to add his head (actually, the silhouette of his head). More message details are related with a wide open mouth brandishing an array of sharp teeth, which affects the shape of his head, and narrowed, angry eyes. Add his nose, too, since he'd look pretty funny without it.

Last, since this is a grizzly not a bald bear, let's suggest some fur. Don't let the amount of fur compete for attention with the teeth. That would undermine the message. Surprisingly, that will happen quicker than you might expect.

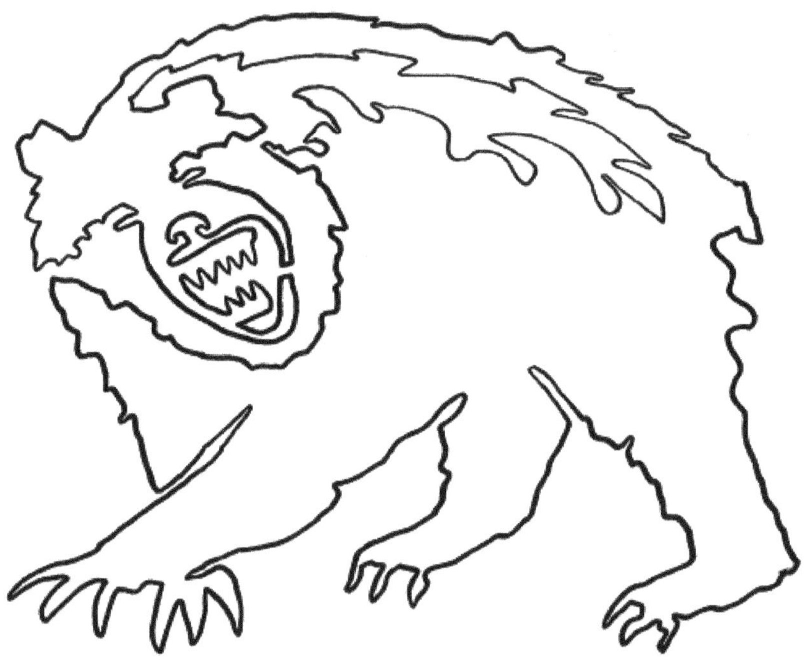

Since we wouldn't expect to find a grizzly bear in a parking lot or on an isolated ice floe, we might want to add some trees and shrubs to make it look like he is in the woods, another important message detail.

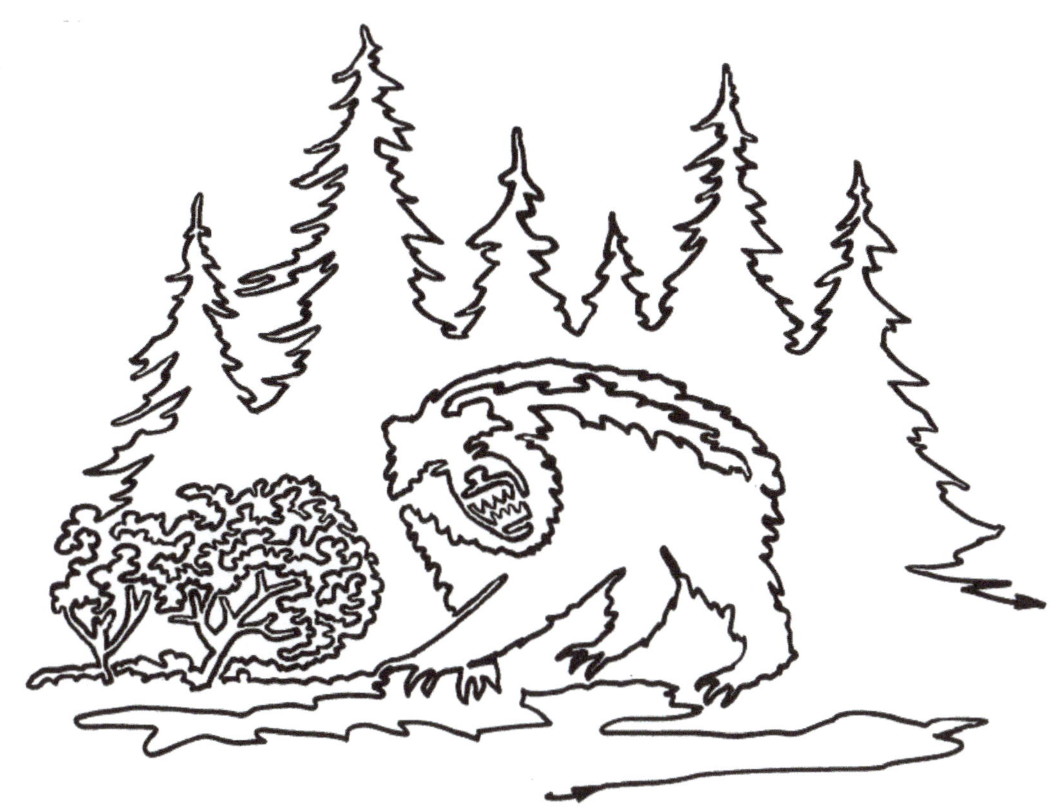

The scene does not need to be photorealistic. For example, there probably are some birds in the trees, some wildflowers covered with butterflies and perhaps some man-made junk in the woods. Including some of these in the scene might increase the realism but wouldn't add anything to the message. It's better to leave them out.

Practice, Practice, Practice

So far you have learned where the power of the line comes from and how to use it to conjure and empower objects. You have also learned that the power of the line is strongest when expressed at the object's silhouette. Anything provided beyond that is simply to add realism and must be chosen with the message in mind.

This suggests a good way to practice and develop your skills. To become conversant with silhouettes, gather up a big pile of magazines and some tracing paper. Trace the silhouettes of the things you see in the magazines. Examine them. Which ones work well for identification and which do not? What would you add to reduce any ambiguities? What does the silhouette tell you about an object's persona and actions? Which characteristics of the line tell you that?

Think of ways you could change the object's message. Redraw the silhouette with line characteristics that support what you want to say. Refer back to the sections on line characteristics and empowerment of objects for ideas on how to influence the viewer's emotions.

Take a sketch book wherever you go. When you have a moment, draw the silhouettes of people, cars, trees, buildings, and anything else that attracts your attention. Examine them and alter them as you did with the silhouettes from the magazines. This will hone your drawing skills as well as strengthen your understanding of the power of the line.

Objects Versus Shapes

At this point, being a painter as well as a line artist, I feel the need to make peace with any aggrieved painters who may still be reading this book. As any painter will tell you, they do not paint objects. They do not paint people. They do not paint trees. They do not paint bears, houses, hands, or any other object. What painters paint are shapes.

Painters say that focusing on objects rather than shapes gives results that look as bad as paint-by-numbers. They are right. They might admit that a shape can be made to represent an object, but that is done only very rarely. Usually you will find objects in a painting that are made up of several shapes and other shapes that represent whole collections of objects. Both conditions typically occur within the same painting; the former at the center of interest and the latter in the background. Deciding which shapes to use to create the impression of objects and groups of objects is a key decision process in composing a painting. All of this is true, and all of it would appear to conflict with this book's focus on objects. However, there is a reason for the difference in focus.

When a painter loads a brush with paint and applies it to a surface, the result is a shape. It has two dimensions, both height and width. A painting necessarily and by definition is a collection of shapes. However, in order to identify and empower whatever the shapes are intended to represent, their characteristics must follow the same rules as those which invoke the power of the line. Even though a painting uses combinations of shapes in its composition, if it is at all representational, various objects must be identifiable. About the only way for shapes to identify an object is to have their edges present enough of the object's silhouette to permit its identification. Thus, the edges of shapes follow the same rules to identify objects as does a line.

Some paintings, of course, don't have any objects at all, only shapes. These are the abstract paintings. However, the same sources of power are at work in the characteristics of shapes as the ones we have been studying at work in the characteristics of the line. For example, consider what was shown in the section on Lines Have Emotional Impact (page 17). Here are some examples of how the same characteristics have the same impact for shapes as they do for lines:

- A bold line attracts attention more powerfully than a thin line or a light line. This is because there is a stronger contrast between the line and the surrounding paper. A bold difference in a shape's color or value (lightness or darkness) relative to those of surrounding shapes has the same effect.

- Vertical, horizontal, and diagonal shapes have the same effects as vertical, horizontal, and diagonal lines. Vertical is more dominant and imposing, horizontal is more restful, and diagonal evokes a sense of energy and action.

- Shapes that curve smoothly are more restful than shapes that change their direction abruptly. The same is true both for the overall shape and for its edges. Shapes with zigzags on their edges are more energetic than shapes with more gentle edges.

- Shapes that are too simple and too regular are less interesting than shapes having more diversity.

- Shapes whose edges appear to converge on an imaginary point give a sense of distance.

When we look beneath the surface, there are many commonalities between the powers at work when painting shapes and those at work when drawing lines. Indeed, a good understanding of the power of the line can help an artist determine the nature of the shapes and their edges that will best communicate the message of the painting. That said, the painter still will want to think in terms of shapes, not objects. We, however, will continue to examine the power of the line by drawing objects, parts of objects, and groups of objects with a focus on what happens at their silhouettes. When our language is lines, rather than shapes, everything we draw necessarily must be the edge of something.

Chapter 4
How to Use a Line to Tell a Story

Now that we know how to conjure and empower objects and to put them into an environment, let's examine ways we can use these tools to tell a story. We'll also examine how the story changes as we change the line's characteristics.

Evoking Excitement and Exhilaration

Suppose we want to share the excitement and exhilaration we feel when we sail a boat on a brisk windy day. The next two drawings show a boat, a man, a seagull, and some water.

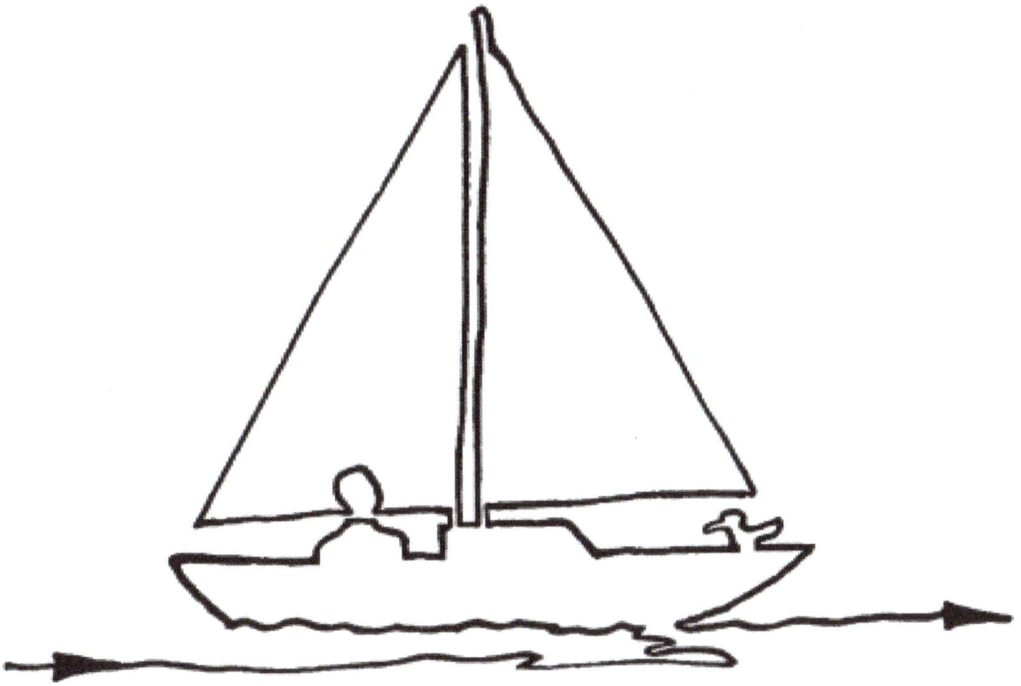

In this version, even if we were inclined to picture ourselves in the boat, we'd probably just want to sail it back to the dock for an early lunch.

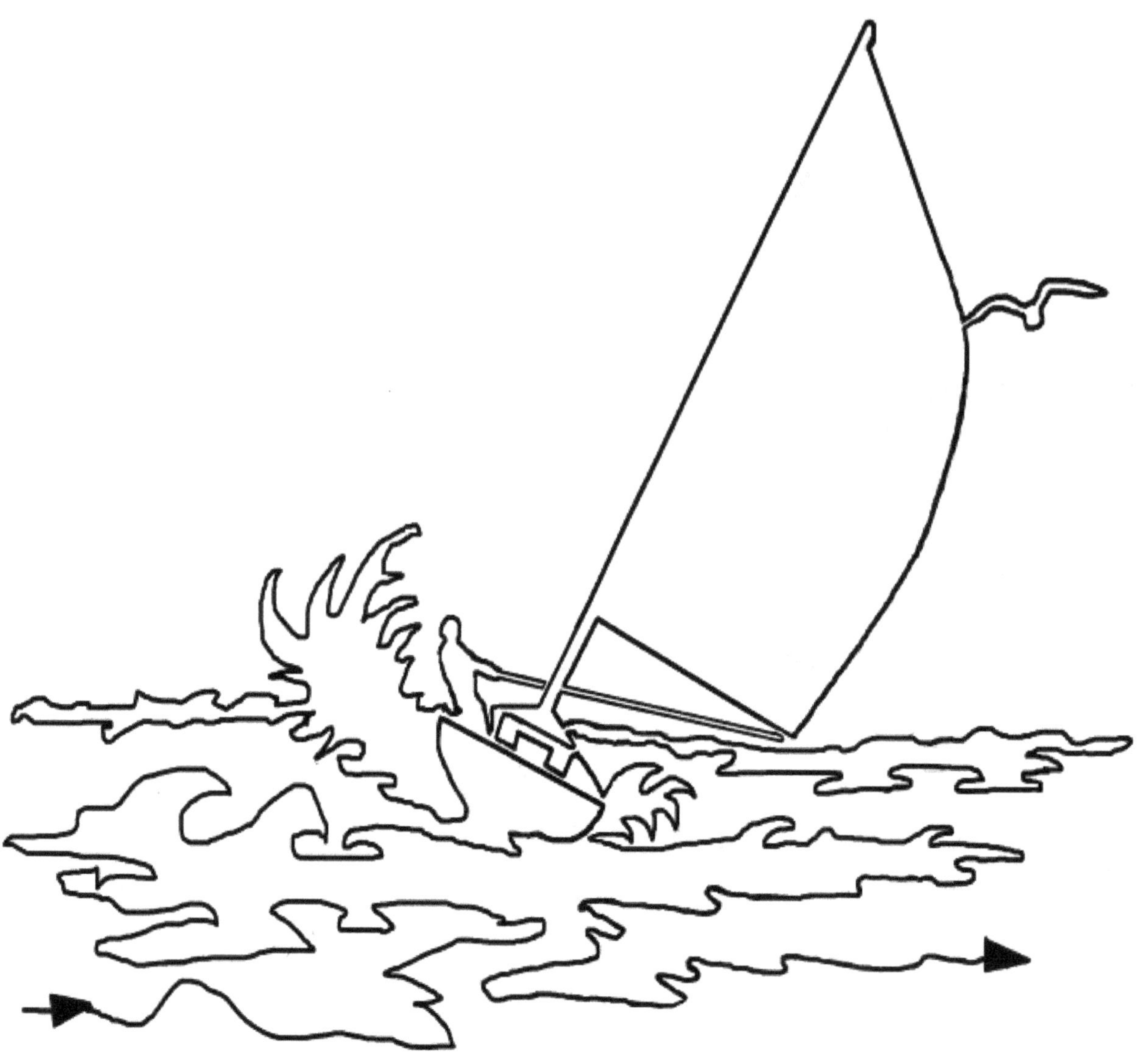

In this version we can almost hear and feel the waves pounding against the hull of the boat as it leaps and bounds beneath us. We can imagine the wind blowing cold spray in our faces. We can appreciate how doing this can be exciting and even exhilarating.

The only difference between the two drawings is the path the line follows as it renders the things we see. As an exercise, write down each characteristic of the line that makes the second version more interesting and exciting than the first.

Here are two groups of people. One group is relaxing at a quiet, sophisticated cocktail party. The only noise is the buzz of conversation with some smooth jazz in the background. The other group is horsing around at the track. They are going to a different party in a little while. It won't be quiet. What things tell us which group is which? Some of the clues are perceived objects and others are the characteristics of the lines.

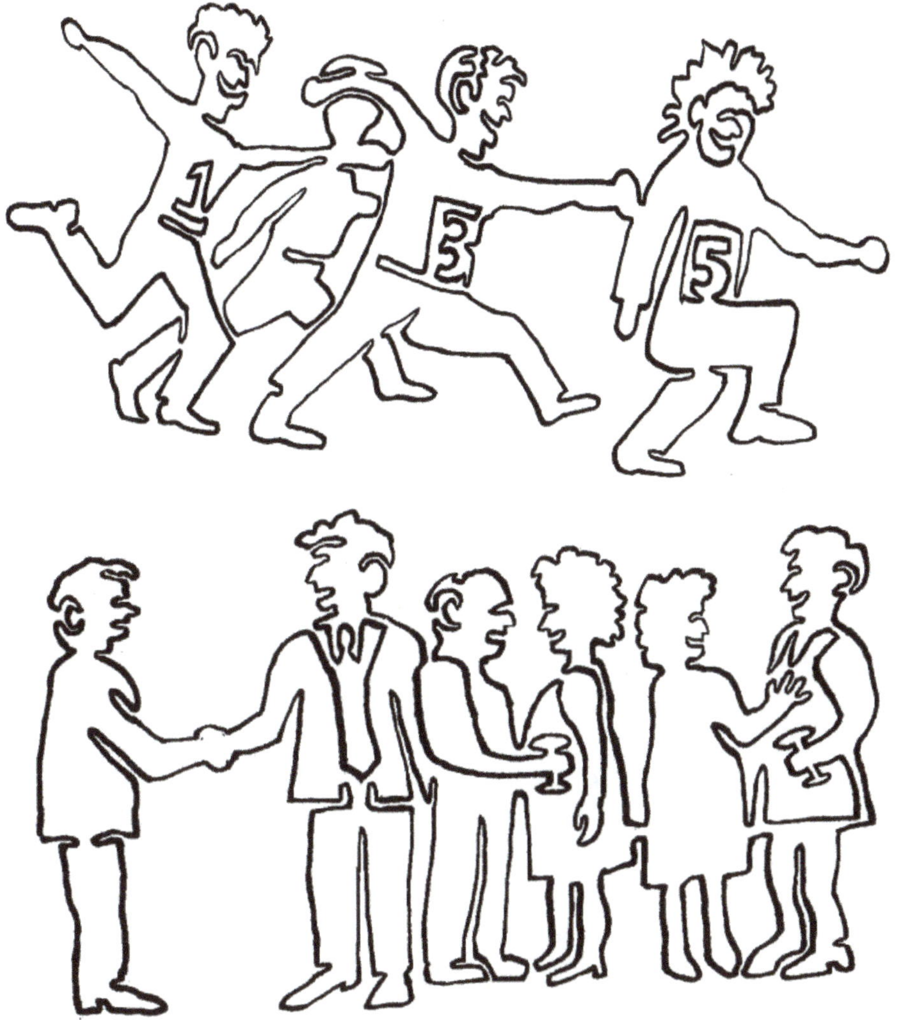

How would your perception of the people at the cocktail party change if they wore pointy hats and some of them were drawn using diagonal lines at various angles or even a few using horizontal lines?

Suppose you want to say something about the discomforts and even dangers faced when people traveled by horse-drawn carriage.

In this example, the only discomfort is if the seat pads are too thin and the only danger is if the coachman goes to sleep and falls off on his head.

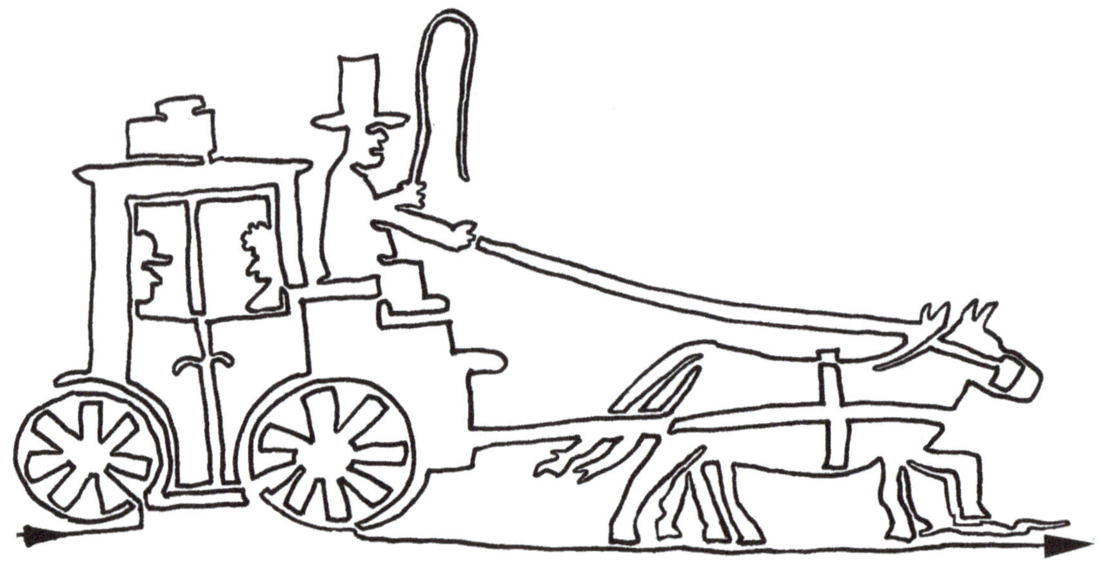

In the version on the next page, the driver is clearly in danger of being thrown from the coach and either breaking his bones or being run over. If the two passengers inside the coach survive the trip, they're going to have some serious bruises by the time they get to where they're going. And they won't have any luggage. They must be pursued by bandits for the driver to race so recklessly!

Both drawings present the same objects: a coach, a driver, two passengers, and two horses. In the first version, there are very few diagonals. There are no zigzag lines, almost no acute angles, and even the corners of the coach are rounded off. The lines are mostly straight and characterless. The second example is loaded with zigzags and has diagonals running all over the place. There's space between the driver and the seat which says he's really bouncing around, not to mention the poor passengers flying around inside the coach. The roadway and its surroundings have lots of bumps, angles, and spiky things.

The characteristics of the line can give us very different messages for the same objects. Of course, if our message had been "going to the opera," the line characteristics of the first drawing might be more appropriate. In that case, adding fancy coach lamps and some wiggly little filigrees would say the occupants of the coach are wealthy.

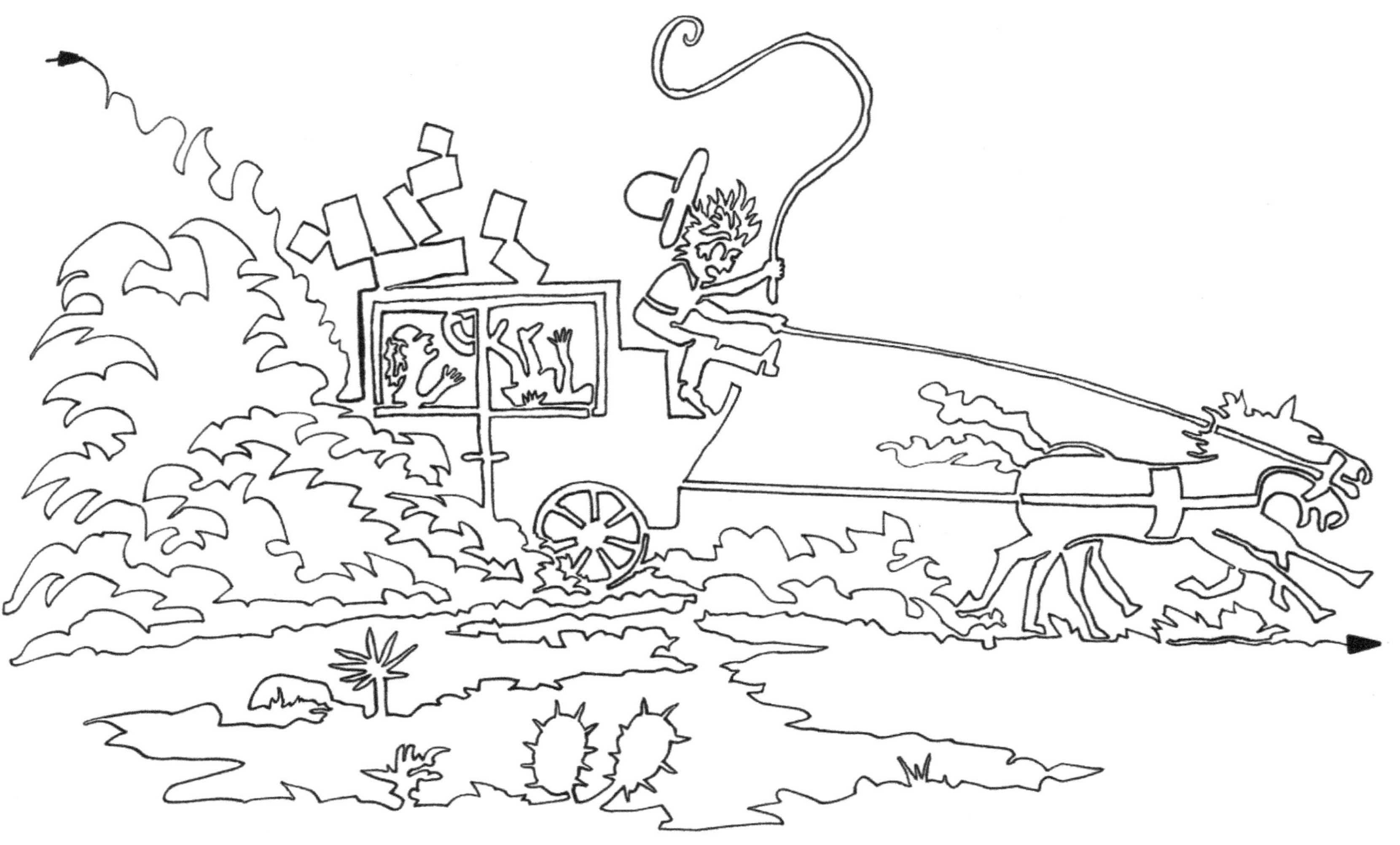

Here are two motorcyclists. One is burning up a dirt track and one is putting along sedately. Who is having the most fun and excitement? What clues convey that information?

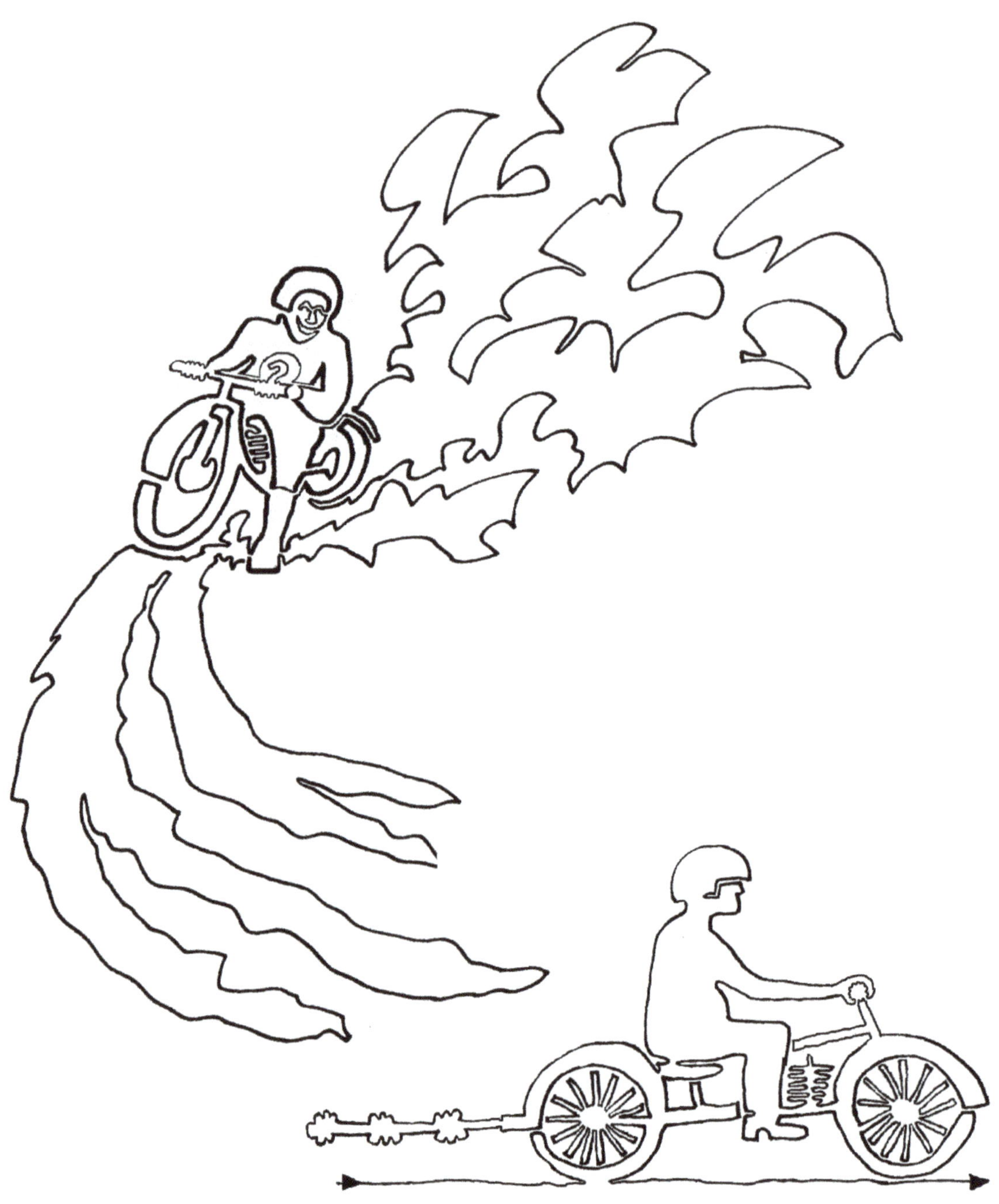

Here's a story about what a dog might feel if he saw a bear on television.

In this version the dog is merely curious. What the heck is that? Is it a fat dog? Perhaps it's just a really ugly cat.

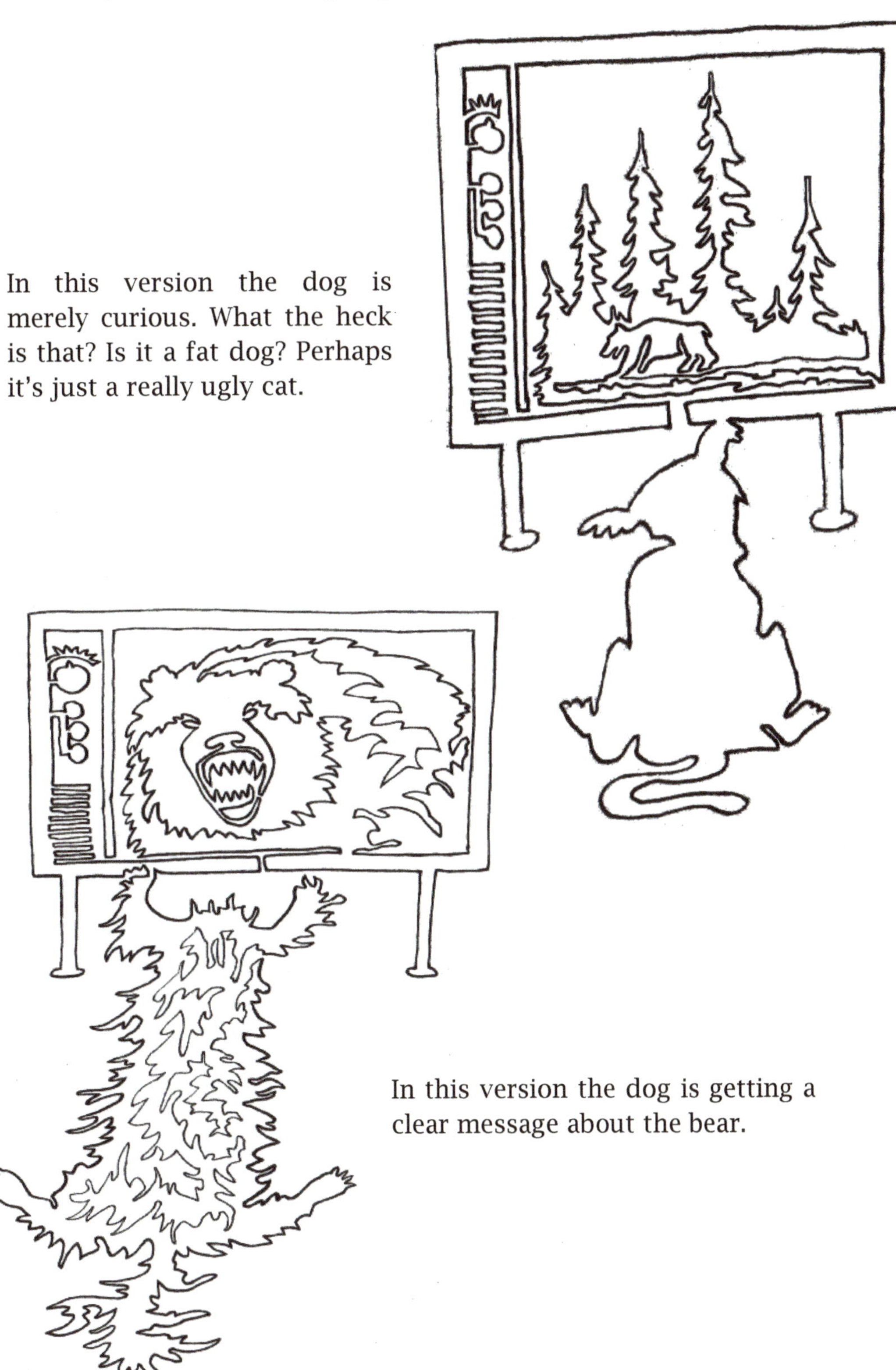

In this version the dog is getting a clear message about the bear.

Which version provokes the biggest chuckle? Is it the strength and nature of the dog's response? What are the line characteristics that tell what both the bear and the dog are feeling? The bear's angry threat is communicated by the shape and angle of his eyes and the show of sharp teeth. They are strengthened by the zigzag lines of the fur outlining his head and his back. To further amplify his threat, the screen shape of the first version, which emphasized the trees and treated the bear as merely one of many objects, has been changed to have the bear filling a panoramic screen. Now he's really in the dog's face. For his part, the dog's ears have flopped wildly up, his legs are splayed, his tail is straight out, and the zigzags in his fur say that it's sticking out from his body. These are all signs of surprise and fear.

In this example, the power of the line is used to convey three very different emotional states on the part of the subjects (curiosity, anger, and fear) and to instill yet a fourth one in the viewer (humor).

Revealing the Inner Man

Here are five different kinds of people nearly all of us know or, at least, have met. This study looks beneath the surface to find the inner man. (Don't read too much into the names. They're just for identification.)

Boris hides his inner self so completely that his outer self is just a mask. But, if you could see the inner man, you'd know that he has a good reason for that. If you fall for the mask, you're in deep trouble.

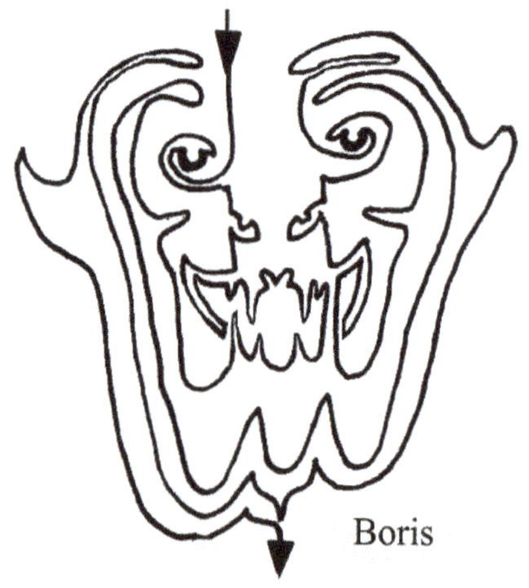

Boris

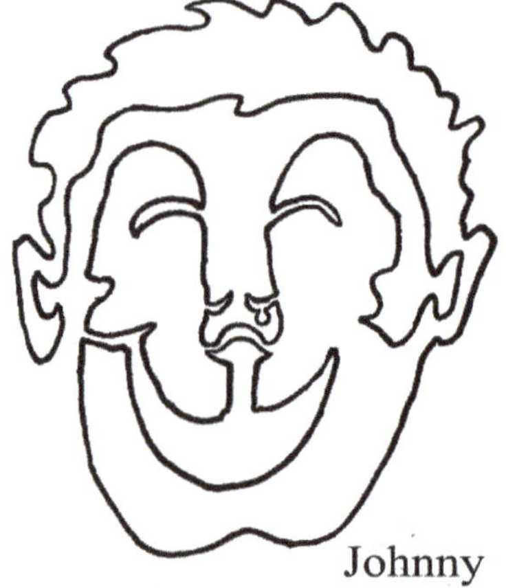

Johnny

Johnny is a guy who doesn't want to burden anyone with his troubles. No matter how down he feels, he'll never let you know that anything is less than wonderful.

Reginald is one of those guys who thinks everyone else is subpar, incompetent, and of questionable morals. We all can recognize him by his judgmental behavior. He'd just die if he thought that anyone even had a clue that deep down inside of him still lives the frightened child he once was who feels totally inadequate and racked with guilt.

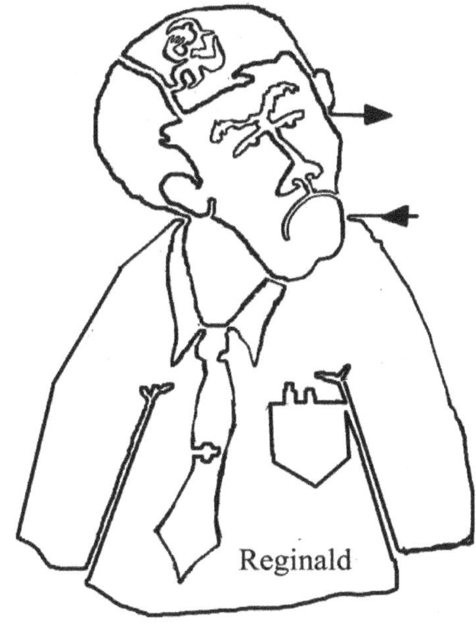
Reginald

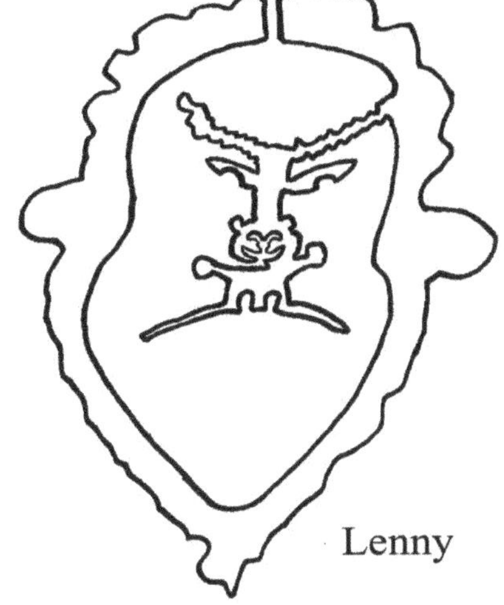
Lenny

Lenny is the perennially grumpy curmudgeon everyone is reluctant to approach simply because he has such a prickly shell. He'd be mortified if he thought anyone knew that inside he's just a big sweet teddy bear yearning for a hug. He's afraid that if he asked for one, we might reject him.

Then there's good old Fred. Nothing ever fazes him. No matter how turbulent, disorderly, chaotic, or even dangerous things get, Fred never loses his cool. He may be frantic with anxiety that things have gotten so out of control, but he'll never let you know that.

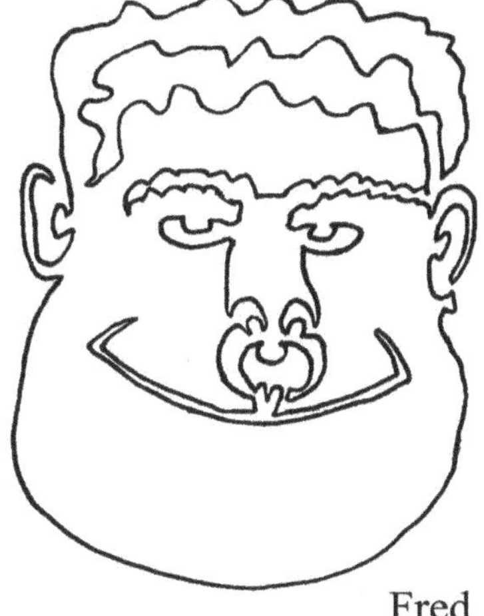
Fred

There's more to this study of the inner man than just how the power of the line works. The message of these drawings also is that you are likely to see one thing if you only take a casual look, but you may find something entirely different if you get up close and pay attention. A lot of people are like that.

Christmas ornaments provide us with an abundance of different subjects to play with. Let's start with some of a gift deliverer (aka Santa Claus) to show how changing the characteristics of the line can change the message from happiness to exhaustion.

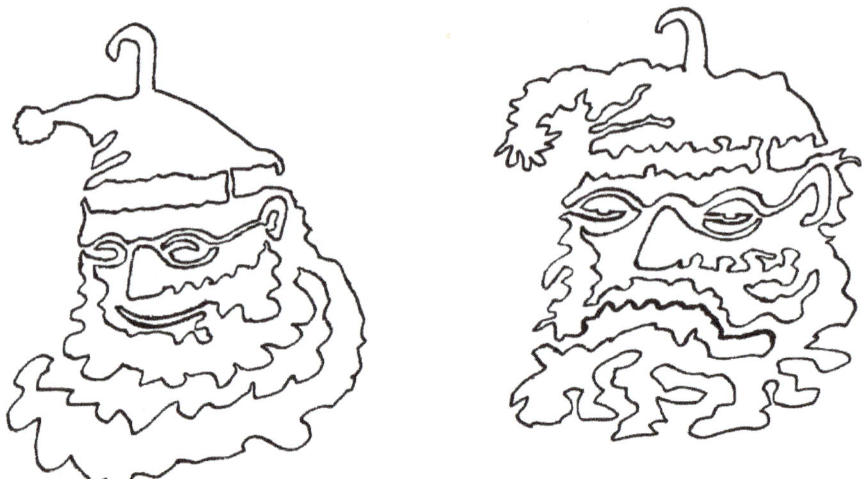

Which ornament shows Santa getting ready to go out to deliver gifts? Which one shows him on the morning after trekking all over the world fighting traffic and trying to find addresses? Which one would you prefer to have on your Christmas tree?

That was fun! Let's do some more! Pay attention now; there's going to be a quiz.

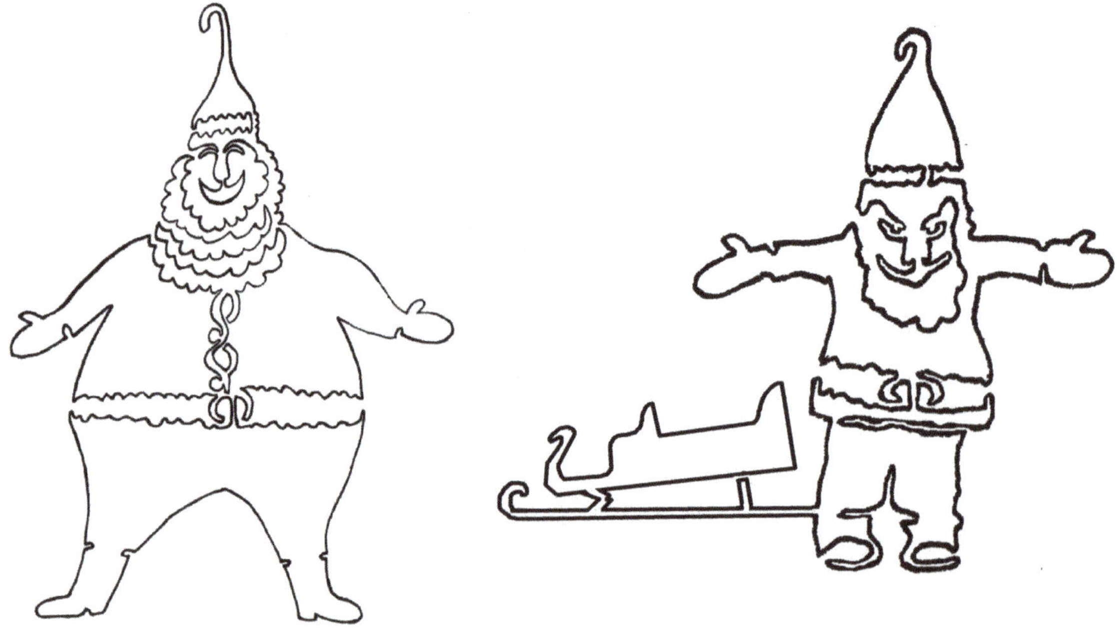

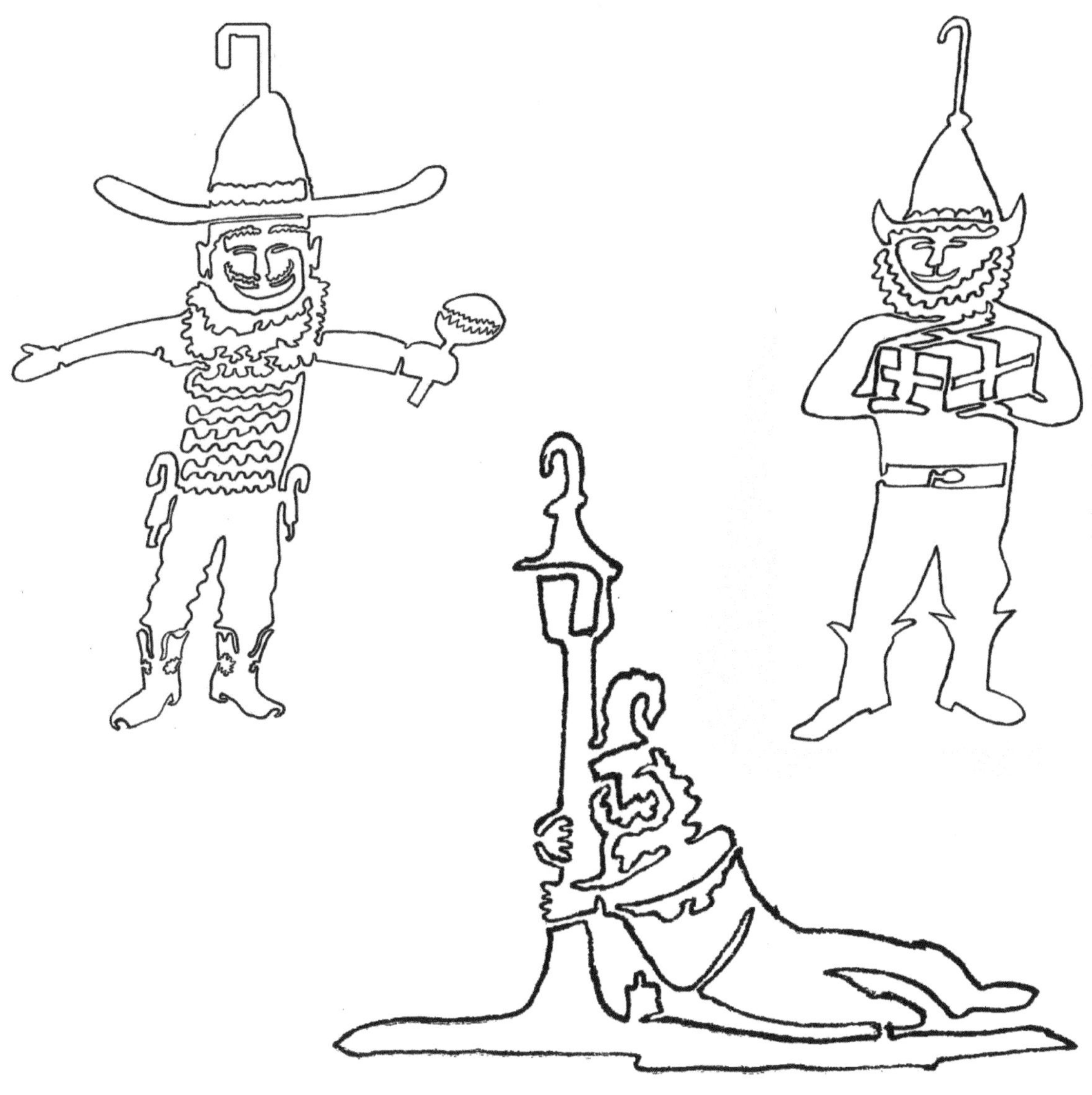

OK! Which Santa is the most traditional jolly Santa? (Hint: He's the one who looks like a candidate for a weight loss program.) Which Santa is most likely to deliver at least some of his gifts in a piñata? Which Santa do you think might want to sell you a used sleigh? Would you buy one from him? Which Santa is really an elf in disguise? Which Santa might have a bit of a drinking problem? He must be one of those department store Santas.

I'll bet you got a 100 on that quiz. Take a moment to carefully examine each Santa to determine what it is about their line characteristics that tells you these things? How do you feel about each of the different Santas?

Since we're on a roll, let's look at some more Christmas ornaments. As you look at each one, make a mental list of which ones would be acceptable for your family Christmas tree. Pay attention, there will be two quizzes on this one!

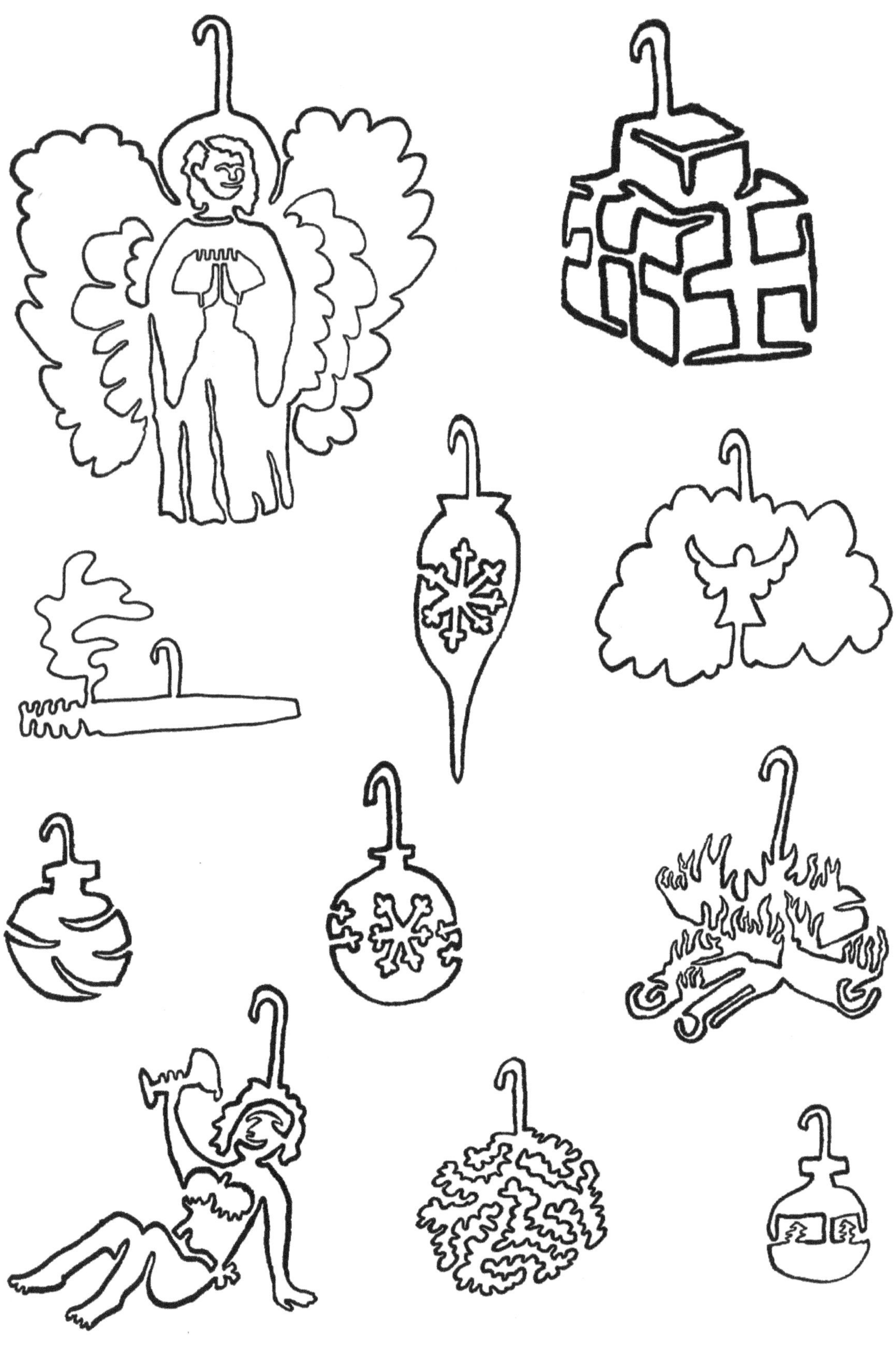

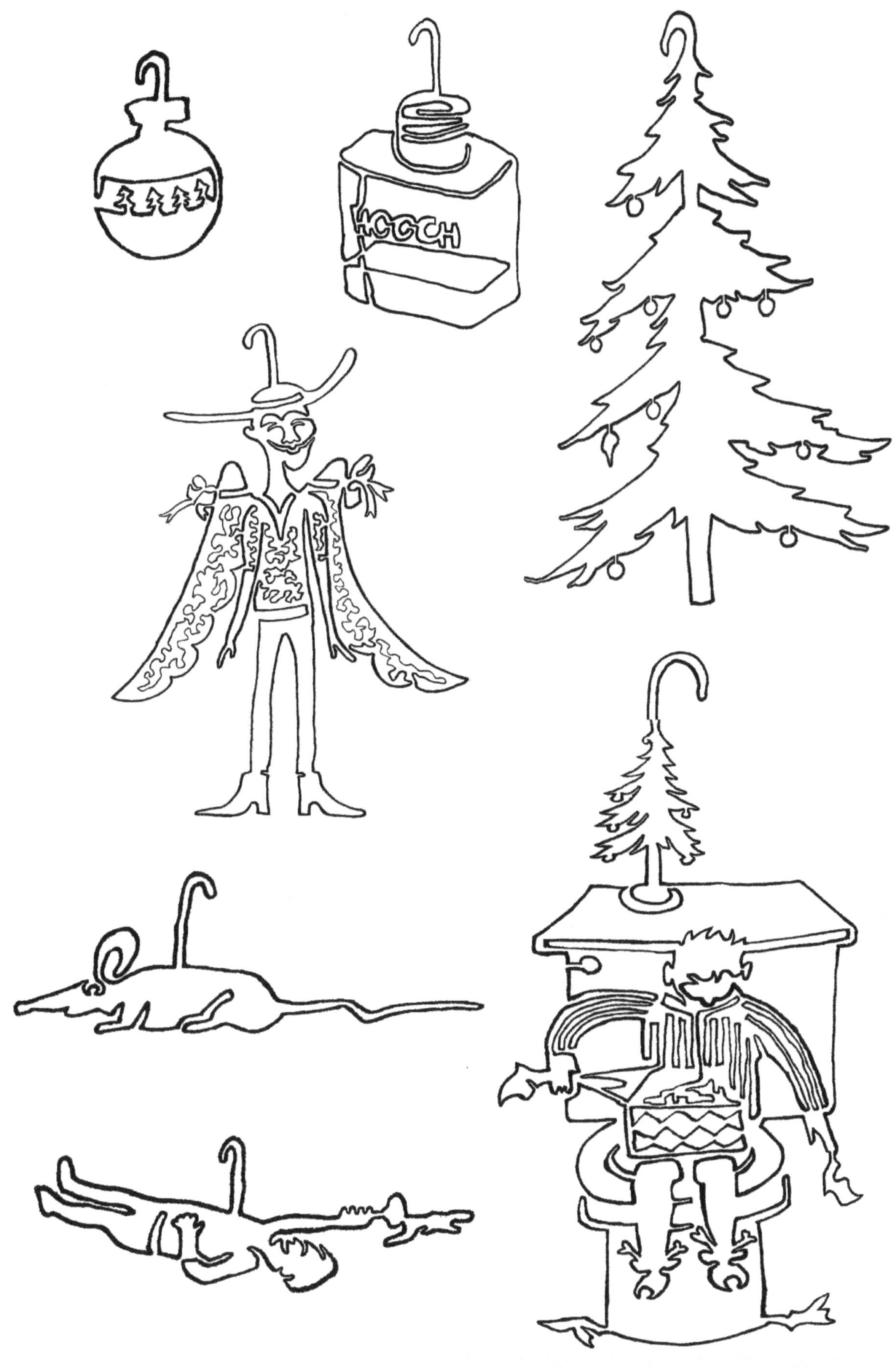
HOOCH

So, which ones made it onto your family's tree? Which ones did not? Was it objects you saw or the line characteristics? Are there any that would become acceptable if they were changed? If so, how would you change them?

Now for the second quiz. Of the ornaments that were not acceptable on your family tree, which ones might you display, just for fun, at an adults-only party? Shame on you!

Changing the Line Changes the Story

Now that you've seen how line characteristics and perceived objects can work together to tell a story, compare this grizzly bear with the one on page 16.

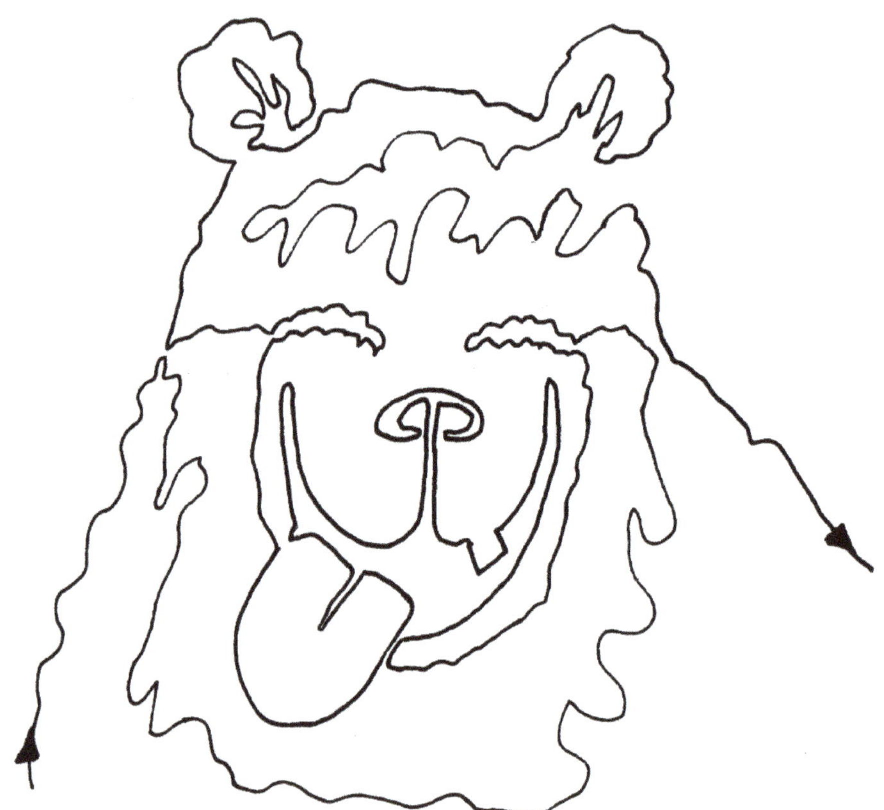

Chapter 5
The Oneliner Gallery

So far, you've seen examples of how perceived objects and line characteristics can work together to tell a story and to affect our feelings and perceptions. Now you're ready to study a whole gallery of Oneliners addressing a wide diversity of subjects to see how it all works together on a larger scale. There are full-page scenes covering everything from indoors to outer space and from realism to abstract.

One purpose of the gallery is simply to provide enjoyment and amusement or, in some cases, shock and distress. But the more important use of the gallery is to develop a well-informed understanding of how and why the line affects you in the way that it does. You now know what to look for. Is it your subconscious response to the objects you see or is it the characteristics of the line? Or is it a mutually supporting combination of the two?

On to the gallery. Have fun, but don't forget to think about what you're seeing, thinking, and feeling and what it is that's causing your reaction.

A Day at Funland in the City

Here are some people trying to get away from it all at Funland in the city. What is the "all" one might want to get away from in the typical urban center? How about crowds, trash, broken pavement, noise, strange-looking people, and long waits in lines. How well are the folks trying to buy cotton candy at Funland doing at getting away from it all? How do they feel about it? How do you feel about it? What is it that makes you feel that way?

Follow the line from its beginning at the lower left corner to where it ends at the upper right. This shows how tortuous the path can get to capture everything needed to carry the message. It also allows you to assure yourself that the line is one uninterrupted line. Everything you see, think, and feel as you look at the drawing is caused by the characteristics of that one line and the path it follows as it moves across the paper. It's all the power of the line.

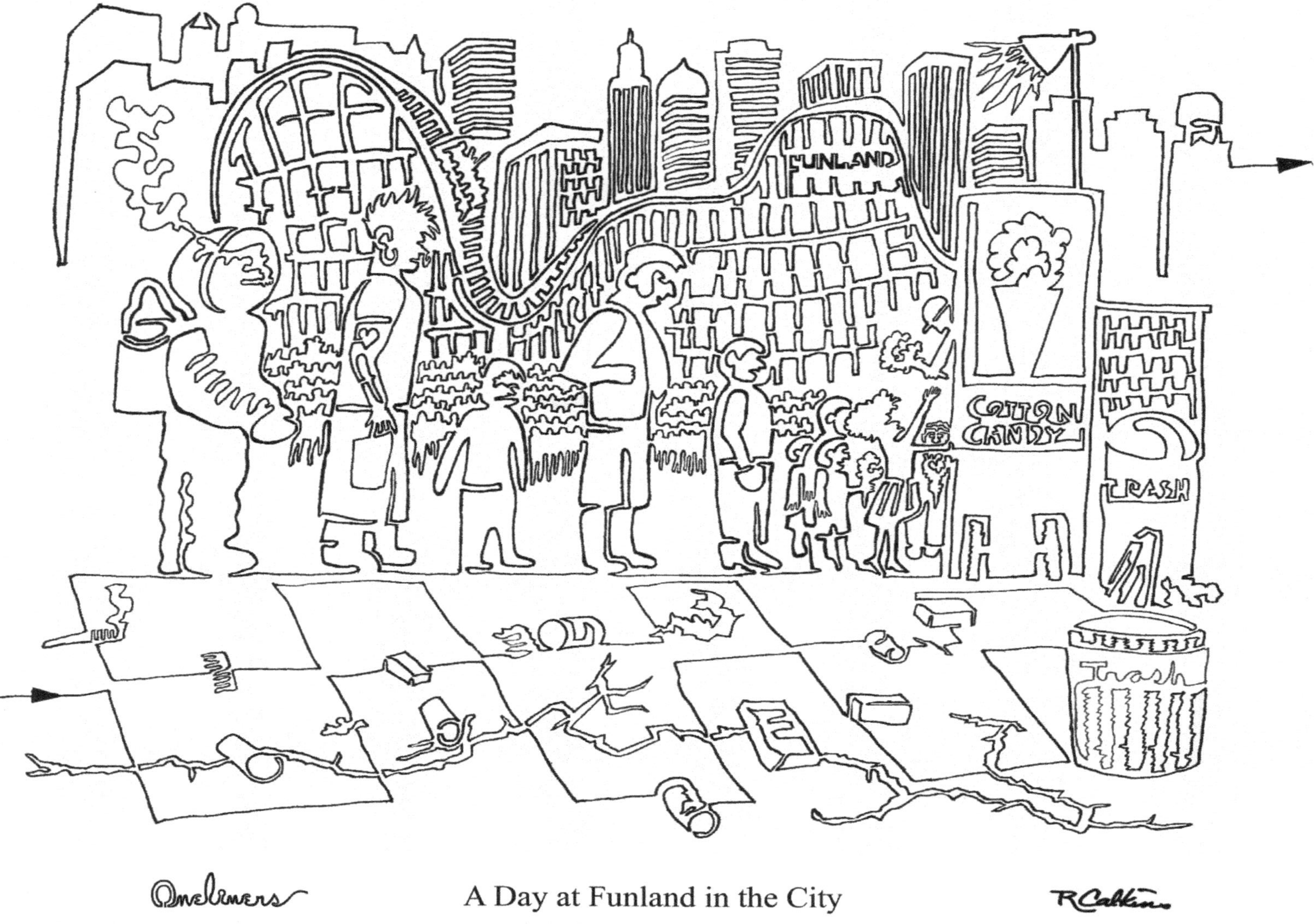

A Day at Funland in the City

These people are hot air ballooning on a hot breezy day in the desert. Can you see the balloons bobbing around and the gondolas swinging back and forth? The parachutist must have jumped from one of them. Do you have a sense of movement, spaciousness, and excitement?

Hey! There's those guys we saw before, racing down that dirt road! They aren't even slowing down to look at the balloons! Where are they going? What are they up to?

The sense of movement in this drawing comes from the zigzag lines in the clouds overhead and in the dust cloud behind the car as well as the diagonal lines used for the balloons.

As an exercise, take a sheet of tracing paper and modify the scene to take out the dust cloud behind the car, put soft and curvy lines in the clouds, make the balloons and gondolas precisely perpendicular, and put everyone's arms at their side. Now the drawing tells a different story.

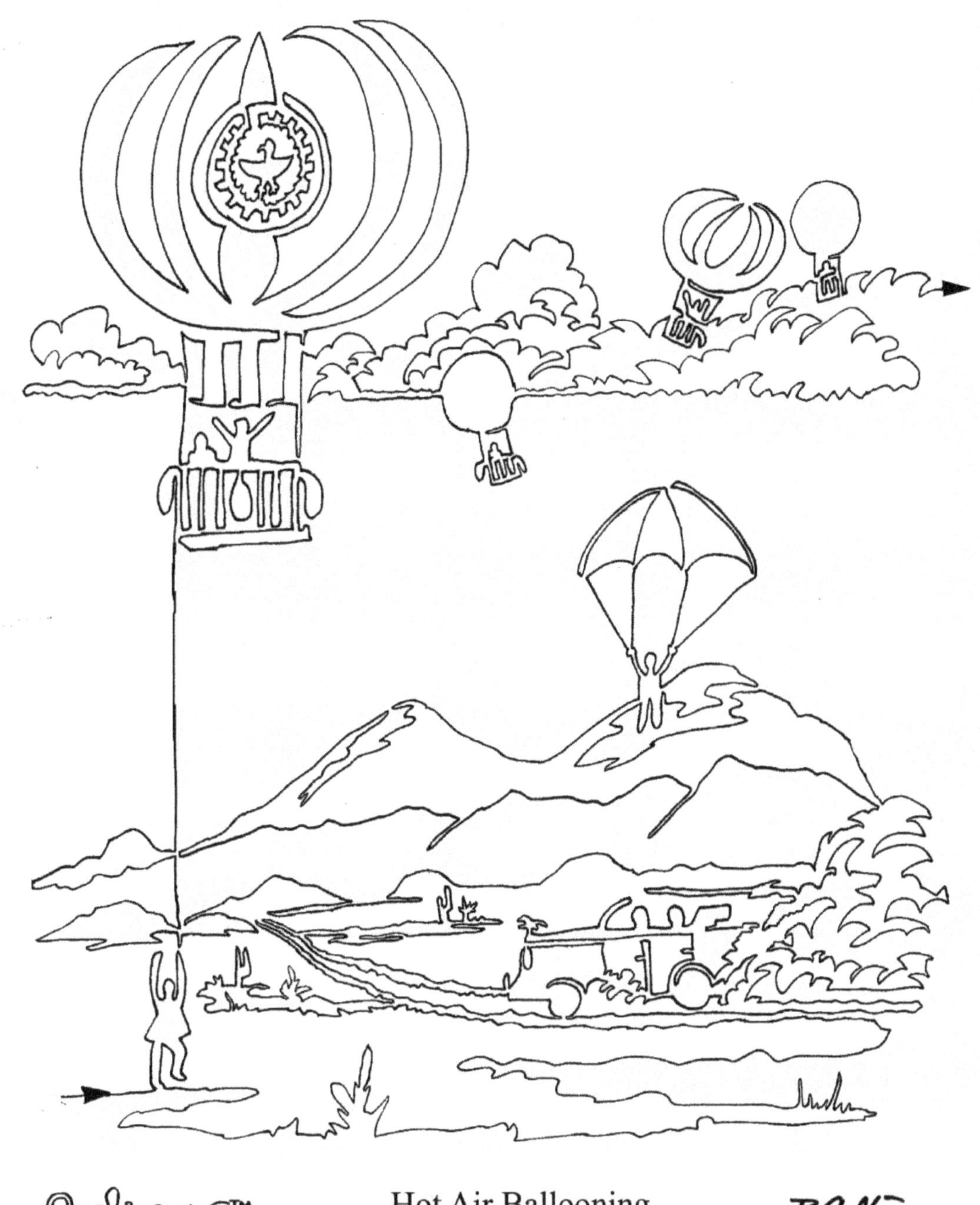

Hot Air Ballooning

Underwater Adventure

Here the power of the line has submerged us deep in the ocean. We won't get wet, we're wearing wet suits. (Or is that dry suits?) There are some other divers across the way keeping a close eye on a shark. The shark seems more interested in that school of fish; at least the divers hope so. Mama and baby whale are watching that shark carefully too. Just to the right of mama whale is something with a lot of teeth that no one wants to meet, including the school of fish.

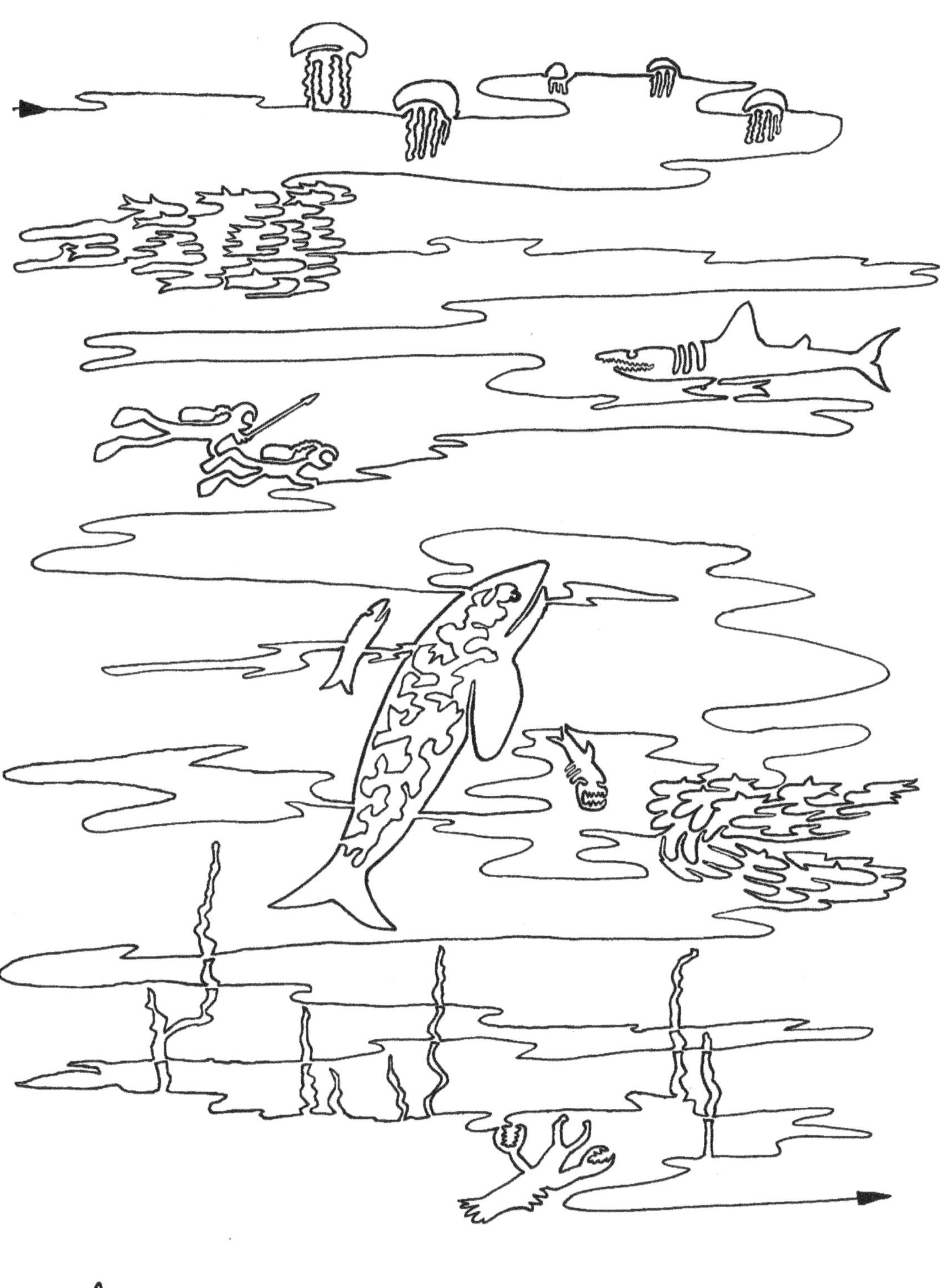

Oneliners   Underwater Adventure   R Calkins

A Sunny Day at the Lighthouse

There's a beautiful lighthouse on Whidbey Island several miles and a ferry ride north of Seattle. It's not occupied any more but is maintained as a historical site. Even though it's in good condition, it always feels a little forlorn. If the lighthouse keeper came back in residence and had some old friends over, it just might warm up a bit.

Cover up the people with your finger and see how the feeling of the scene changes. If you also cover up the birds and the boat, the scene becomes even more lonely.

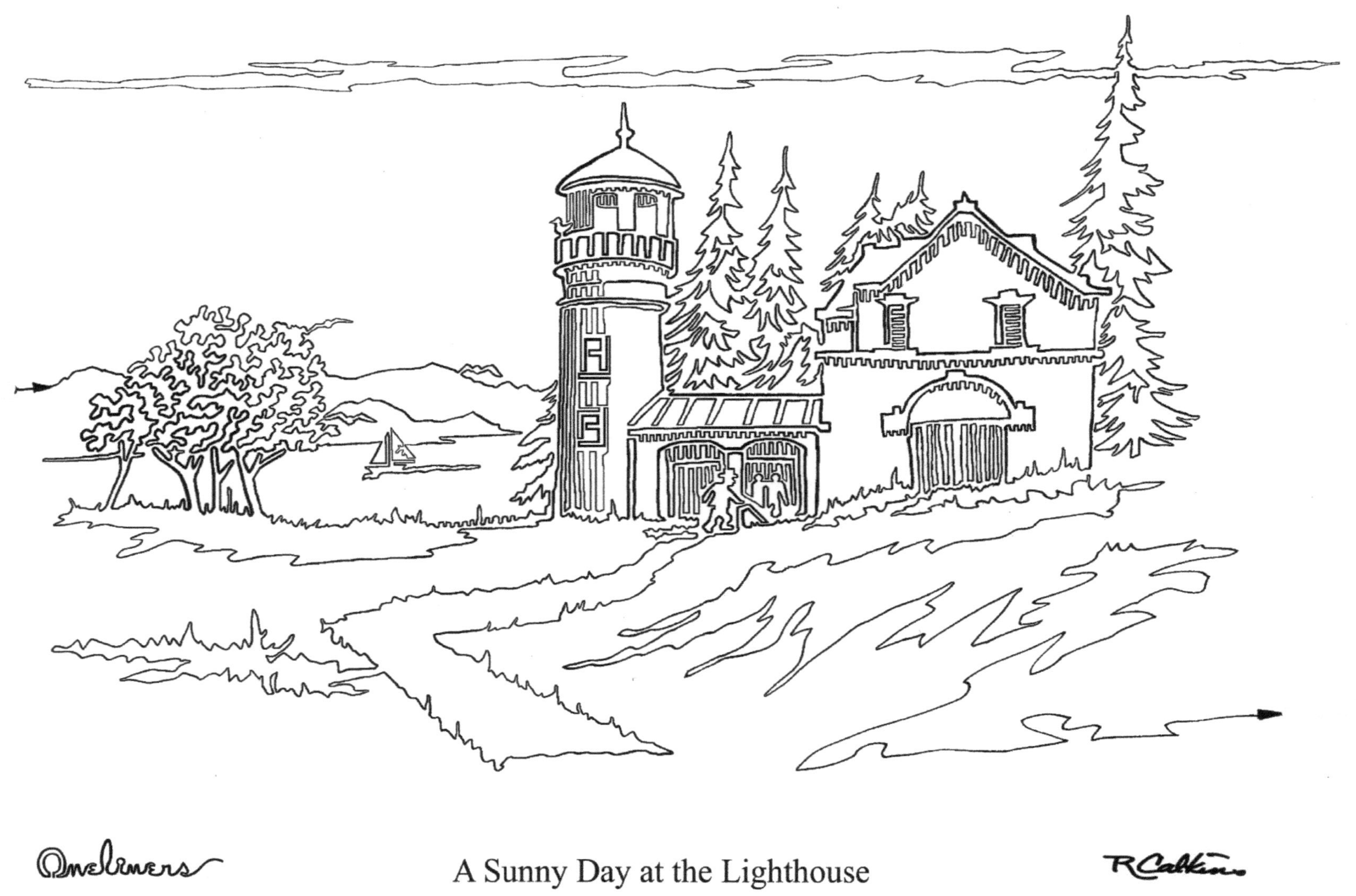

A Sunny Day at the Lighthouse

Uninvited Guests

This is one of those vinyl Italian-style tablecloths set for a snack with wine, cheese, and fruit. Whoever is planning to enjoy it apparently has wandered off, maybe to answer the phone. Do you think he's going to be happy when he gets back? No? What makes you say that? How do you feel about what you see? Are you ready to dig in?

Note that the sides of the squares on the tablecloth do not converge on an imaginary point. They are parallel with each other. This distorts the perspective, giving the table a slightly off-kilter look, adding to your sense of unease. The subject matter and the line characteristics combine to amplify the message.

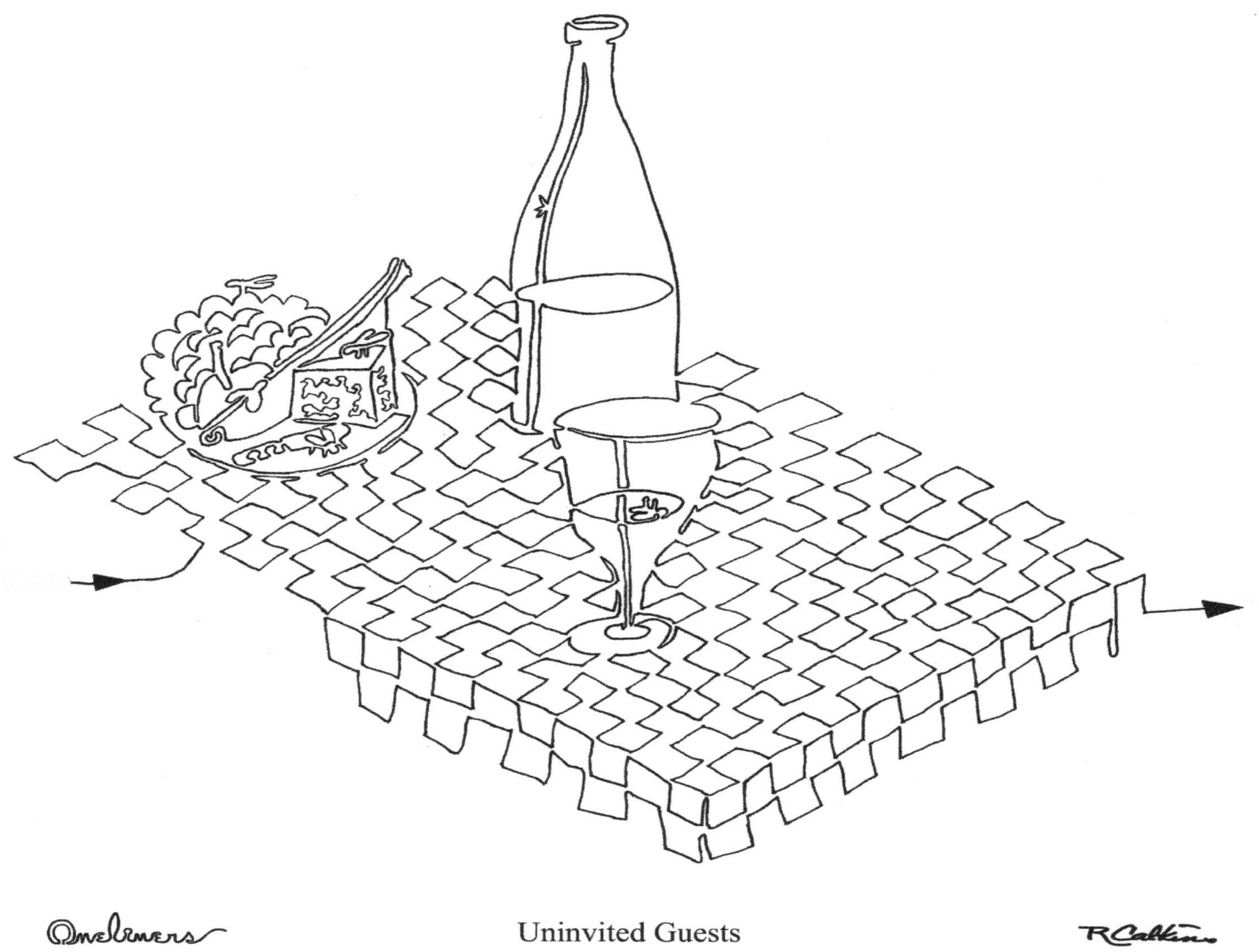

Uninvited Guests

Through the Darking Woods . . . Just In Time

When you were young, did you ever walk through the woods or a park just as it was getting really dark? Did your imagination start to populate the woods with scary things?

Of course, now you know that the rustling you heard in the underbrush was just a squirrel hiding a nut. As grownups, we know there's really nothing out there in the dark that would harm us.

In this drawing, the children have made it into town, but we're still in the woods. It's really getting dark in here and I hear some strange sounds. Maybe we should catch up to the kids . . . just to look after them. Oh kids. Oh kids! Wait up!!

To make this a night scene, it was necessary to simulate darkness within which most things are hidden but the dangerous creatures can still be discerned. However, the simulated darkness needs to be less interesting so it doesn't overwhelm the sinister objects that carry the message. Thus, the line segments that simulate darkness are all straight (but not ruler straight), parallel, and uniformly spaced. They also are diagonal and not precisely uniform, which makes the darkness vibrate with the potential for action. Consider how the scene would feel if all the darkness line segments were vertical. How would it feel if they were all horizontal? How would the scene feel if the darkness line segments were drawn absolutely straight with a ruler and with absolute precision in their spacing and angle?

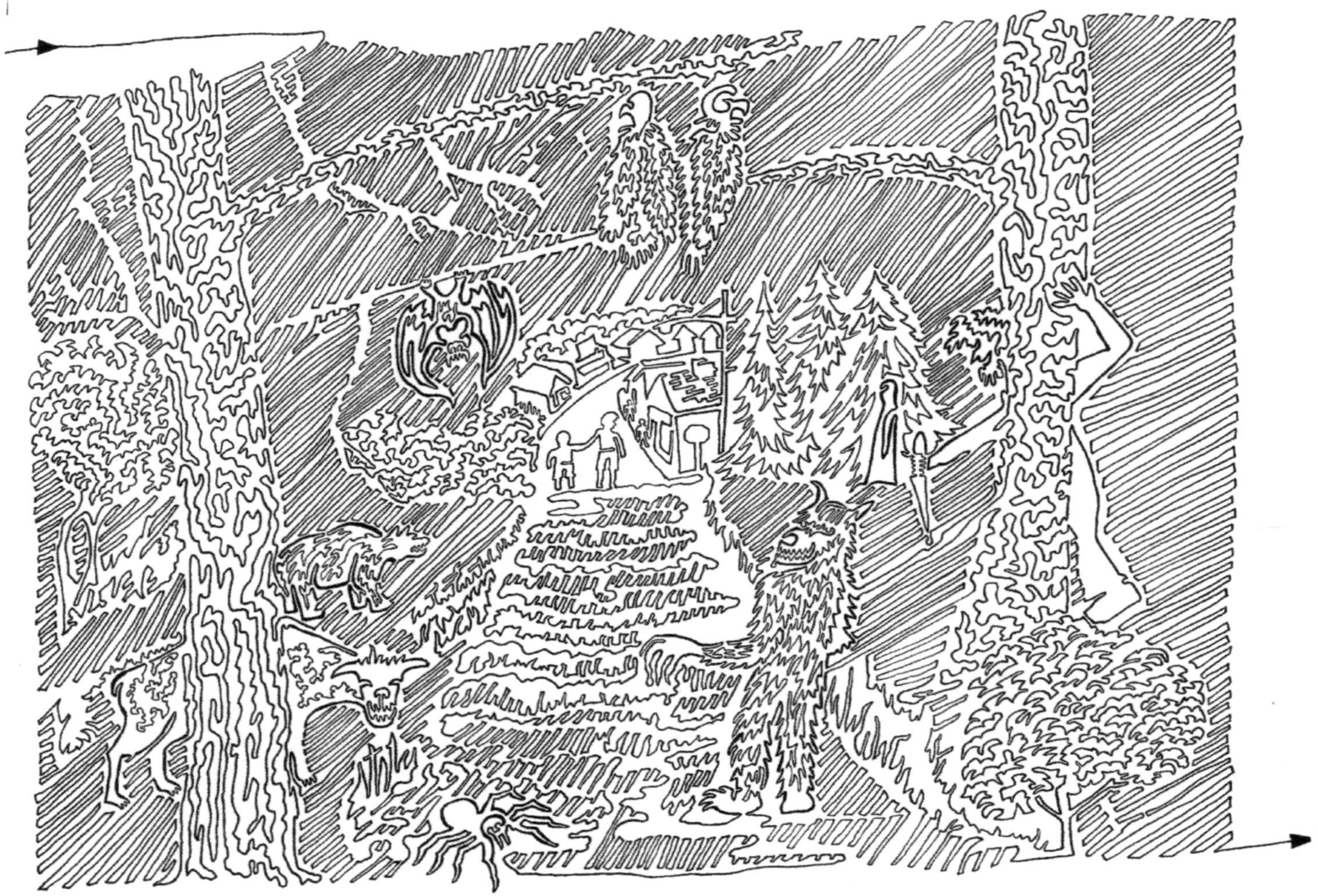

Through the Darking Woods ... Just in Time

The Christmas Spider at Work

With the power of the line, we can get a close up look at the Christmas Spider at work. The ornaments he hangs are made of ice crystals and usually are too small to see individually. We can only see them when they are clustered into large groups. On cold, clear, icy days he hangs them all over the place - on wires, branches, twigs, and especially all over his web.

What?! You've never heard of the Christmas Spider? Haven't you ever been out on a clear, icy day during Christmas season and seen the sun glisten on the flowers, twigs, and spider webs? What you saw was the sunlight reflecting off of the thousands of tiny crystal ornaments hung by the Christmas Spider. If you've ever seen that, you've seen the work of the Christmas Spider.

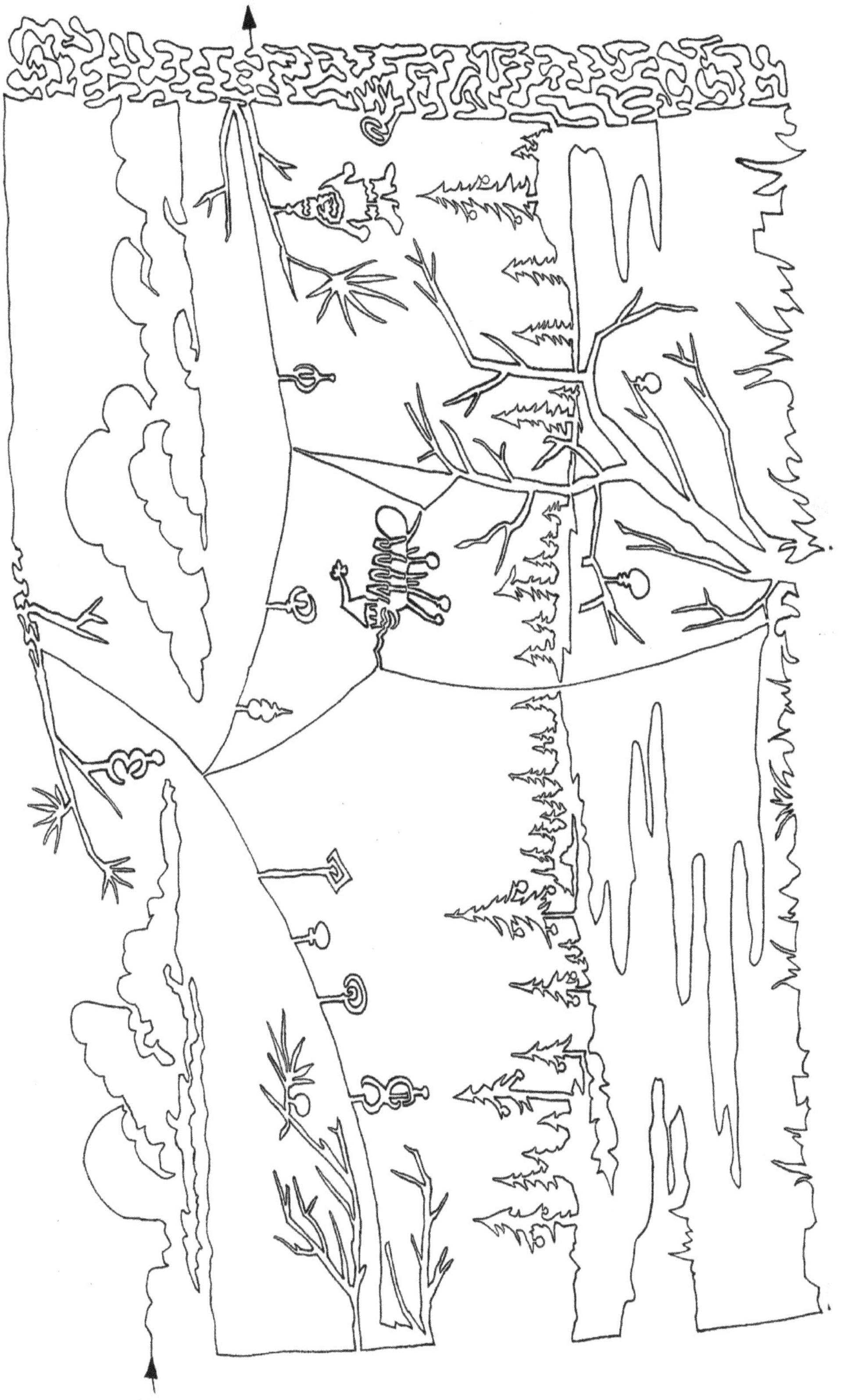

OneLiners™

The Christmas Spider at Work

R Calkins

Sun Day in Seattle

Everyone knows the Pacific Northwest doesn't get a lot of sunshine. So when the sun does come out, just imagine what happens.

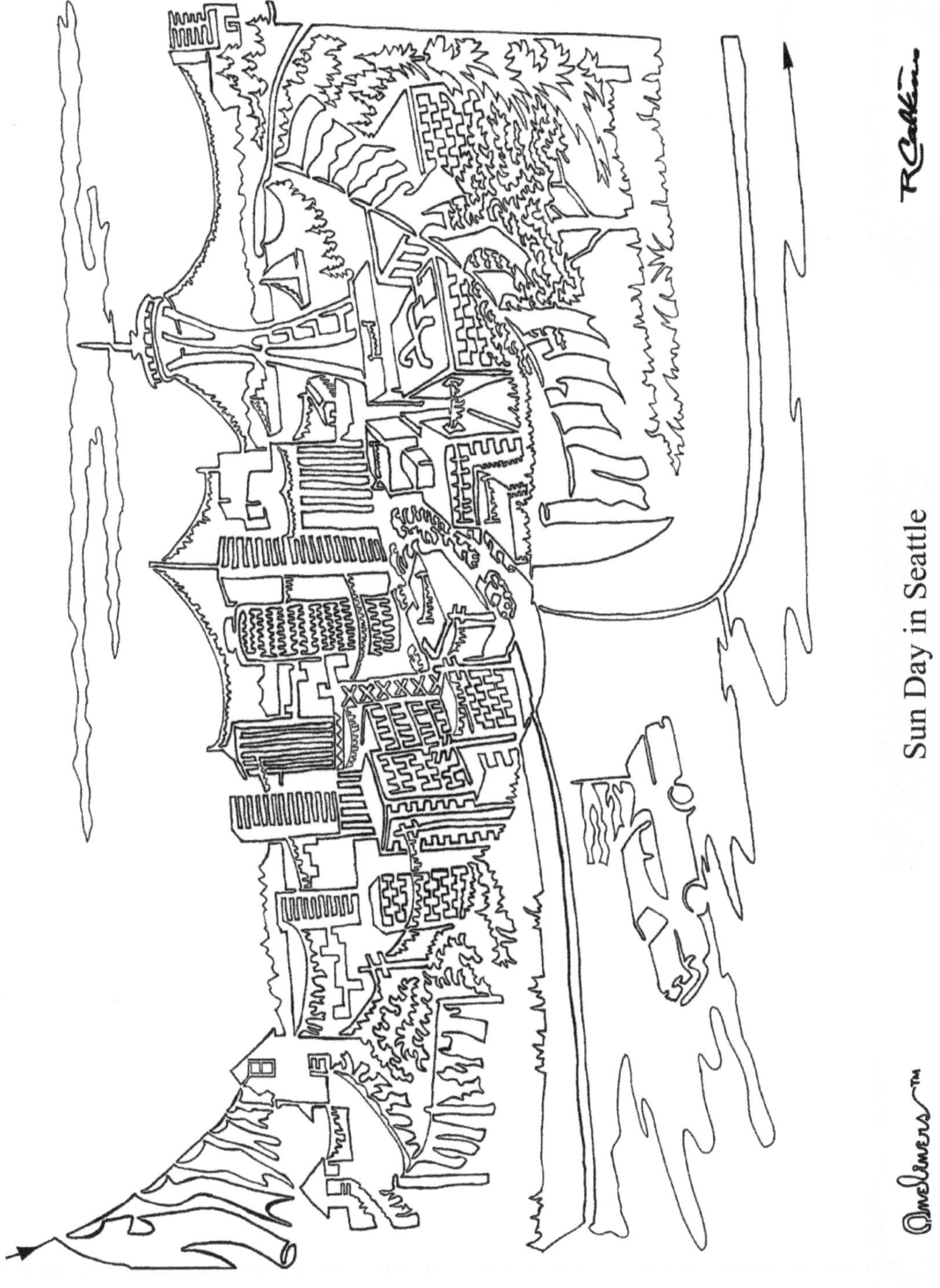

Sun Day in Seattle

Potted Plants

Here's a still life of some potted plants. It's not too hard to figure out how they managed to get potted. What is it about the line's characteristics and some of the objects that tells us the plants are out of sorts?

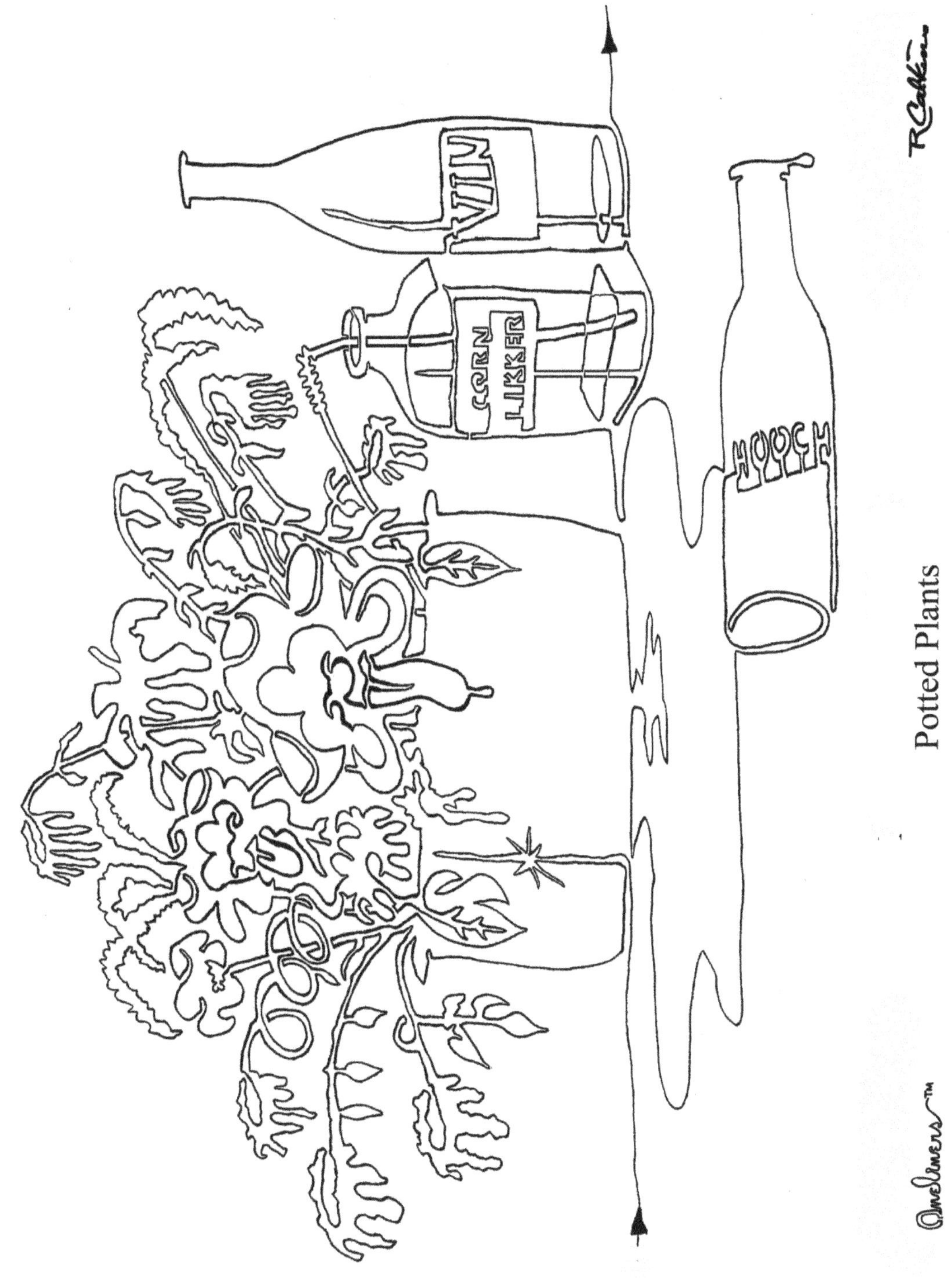

Potted Plants

This is the most abstract drawing of the collection. You can study this drawing to good effect at least three different ways.

One way is simply to wander visually around the drawing to examine each of the symbols that are buried in the catacombs. What does each one convey to you? What do you feel about it and why?

Another way is to follow the line from where it starts at the upper left side of the drawing to where it ends on the middle right side. You'll find that it goes back and forth a lot. This is because the more you have in a Oneliner, the harder it is to get from one object to another without having to cross over another part of the line. What you have to do is wander off and do parts of some other objects until you get around to where you can finish the rest of what you were working on. This is why it pays to do more than one version of a subject when drawing Oneliners. Some starting points and approaches will work better than others. And all of them will make you think about what to put in and what to leave out. Deciding well on what to leave out helps you navigate the drawing with the least amount of damage to your intent.

The third way to enjoy the drawing is to put on your pith helmet, get out your lantern and follow the tunnels through the catacombs to experience the story there. On the far left side of the drawing, enter the catacombs and follow the stairway down to the tunnels. Continue down to the locked chest full of secret treasure. Avoid the curvy cul-de-sac and continue down the tunnel to the branch that goes to the bat cave. You can go up that branch and visit with the bat. Step carefully; he's not a good housekeeper.

Go back down to the main tunnel and follow it to the small chamber with a floating balloon. The balloon has a cryptic "A" on it. What does it mean? I don't know; it's a secret. Go past the balloon and continue up the stairs. At the second landing you will come to an opening back at ground level. Stepping through the opening, you'll find yourself on a long flat surface. Uh-oh! You're standing in the runway! It's used to fly archeologists and dignitaries in to see the catacombs.

Quick, cross to the other side of the runway and re-enter the catacombs. You will find yourself on a landing with stairs going back down into the catacombs on both sides. If you take the stairs to the left, you will find the grotto of the bodiless head. He's very grumpy at not having a body and doesn't say very much. Maybe you can open him up a bit.

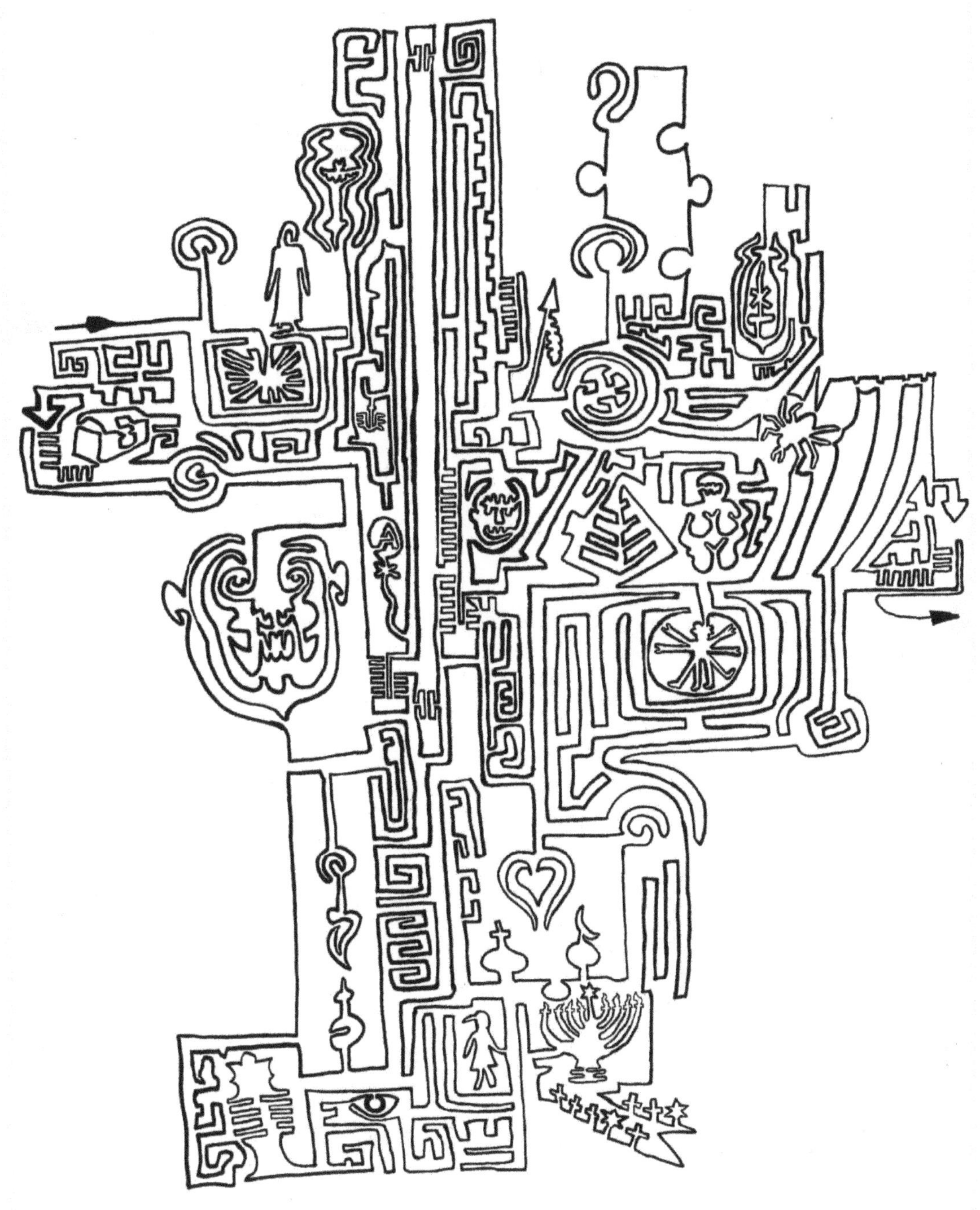

The Catacombs of Secrets and Symbols

After trying to talk with the bodiless head, go back to the landing and take the stairs down the other side. At the bottom of the stairs, you'll come to an opening with tunnels in both directions. If you go to the right, you'll just get lost in a dead-end maze. If you go to the left, there's a quick turn to the right to the bottom of an Egyptian pyramid. You can't go inside it from here, so just go up alongside of it past the pyramid to where the tunnel ends at a long curved wall. Following the curved wall to the left, you come to a Native American ceremonial spear with its feather totem. To your right is an opening into a circular tunnel. If you follow the tunnel to the right, you will eventually find your way up to the chamber of innies and outies. I don't know how they got that way, but I thought you might find them interesting.

Now trace your way back to the end of the tunnel you used to get past the pyramid. Passing the end of that tunnel, continue along the curved wall until it straightens out into a long, narrow tunnel. Walking down it in the gloom of your flickering lantern, you see some glittering orbs ahead. Aaagh! Those are big eyes! It's the dreaded Spider of the Catacombs! Quick, run down the tunnel to the right and get around the corner!

Whew! That was close. Wandering on you will meet the Lady of Fertility. Have a little chat with her and then climb down inside the pyramid. There are lots of tunnels in there, but they are all empty. Apparently the catacombs are not secret enough to thwart the tomb robbers.

The last tunnel to explore goes inside the Vitruvian Man's head where you can look at the world through his eyes. He is widely believed to be a self-portrait of Da Vinci, so it might be a very interesting view. After that, head out the same way you came in. Did you remember to leave a trail of bread crumbs?

There are lots of other entrances into the catacombs. Seek each one out and see where it leads. Some of the tunnels lead to dead ends and others open into new underground vistas.

Just think, you had this entire adventure just because of the path followed by a line as it wanders across the paper. If you hold the page at a distance, you can see that the whole drawing is a type of composition called a cruciform, a frequently used framework for abstract paintings. It subtly invokes a sense of importance, reverence, and mystery that lends gravitas to the shapes and colors of the abstract.

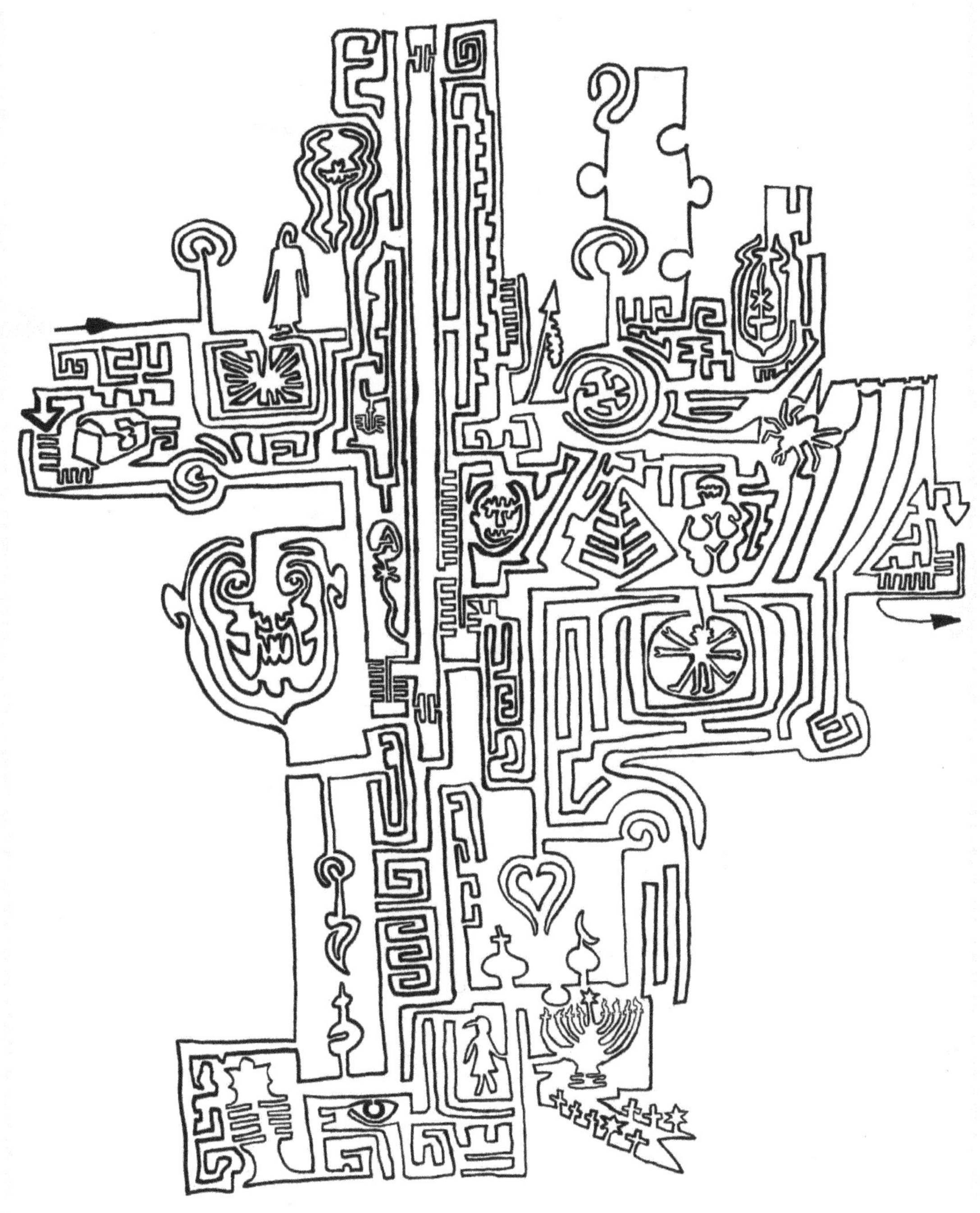

The Catacombs of Secrets and Symbols

While there are lines going off in all directions, the overwhelming line dominance is vertical. The runway and the tunnels below it split the full height of the drawing with a strong vertical statement. The spider's web, both sides of the Vitruvian Man, and several other areas present unbroken vertical line segments that are longer than just about any of the horizontal segments. Remember the psychological message of vertical: proud, serious, upright, unbending, commands respect, can even be a bit intimidating. These catacombs are serious business. You never know what you might encounter around the next bend. It might be dangerous.

Note that none of the lines are ruler straight. All have the slightly random look of hand drawing which imparts the sense that these catacombs are ancient and carved out of the rock by hand with crude implements.

When you drag your pen across the paper, the line that results can speak in many ways.

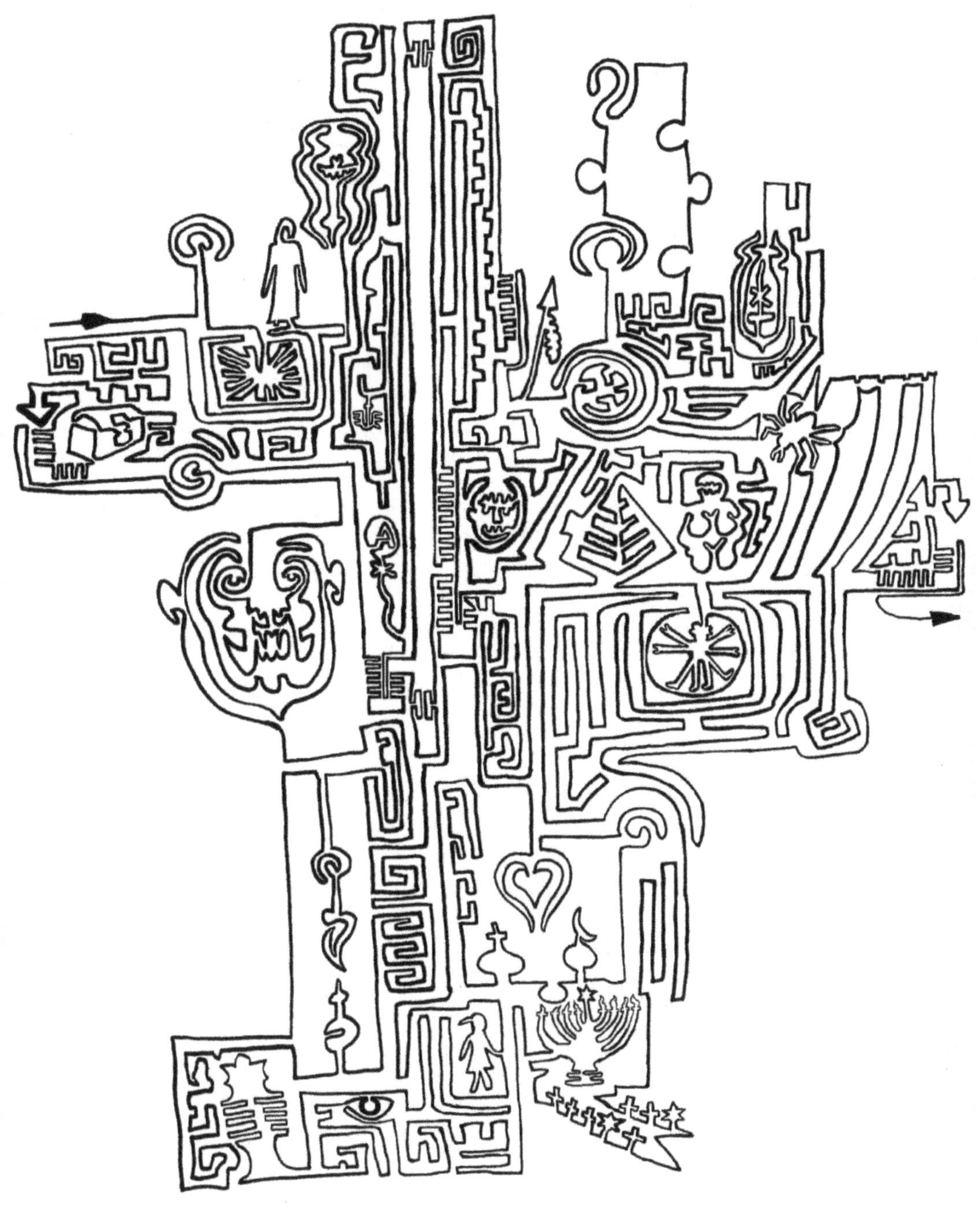

Onelerners — The Catacombs of Secrets and Symbols   R Calkins

Intellectual Cliff Climbing

Here are a couple of rock climbers on a sheer cliff using the occasional narrow ledges and cracks in the rock formation to ascend. They even climb places where the rock hangs out over their heads, driving pitons into the cracks and hanging from them on ropes. The rope will always be fastened securely to the rock face, except for a brief moment while the pitons are being moved. If one of the climbers happens to fall right then, they'll both go down together. That's called the buddy system.

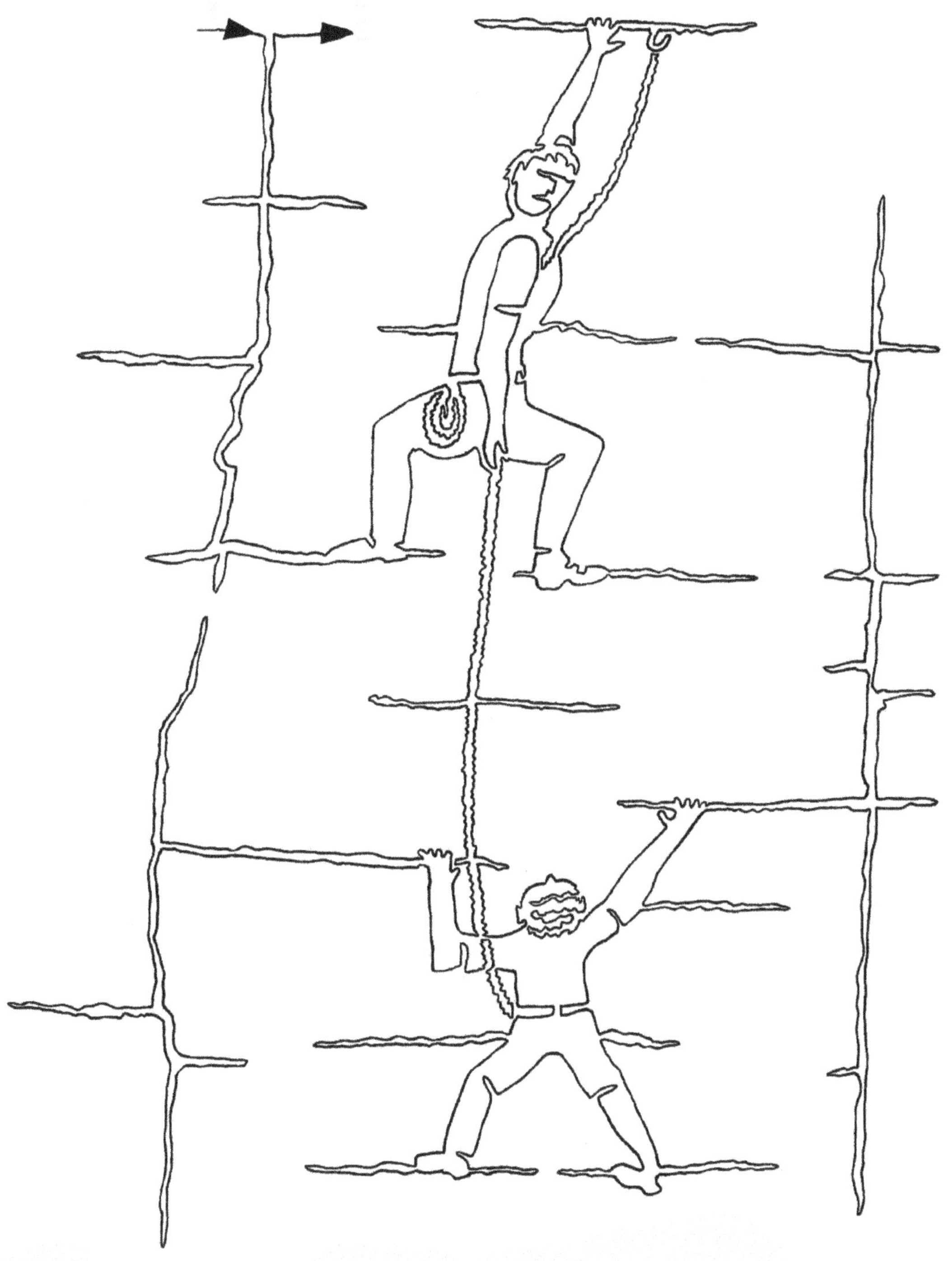

Intellectual Cliff Climbing

Visceral Cliff Climbing

Here are the same two climbers in the same positions hanging on the same tiny ledges on the cliff. But this vantage point triggers an instinctive program that shouts "Danger! Danger!"

The line orientation in this drawing depicts the subject in a way that conveys just how scary and dangerous it is to climb a vertical cliff hanging on tiny ledges and crevices. The relative size of familiar objects at the bottom of the cliff -- evergreen trees, people, a tent, and a vehicle -- reinforce the feeling of great height.

Note that the line segments connecting all the objects on the ground are shaped to hint at rocks and weeds but are thinner than those used to depict the objects. That tells our subconscious those parts of the line are just background information. They inform us about the terrain without competing with our identification of the trees, people, tent, and vehicle. It's the identifiable objects that support the message of great height.

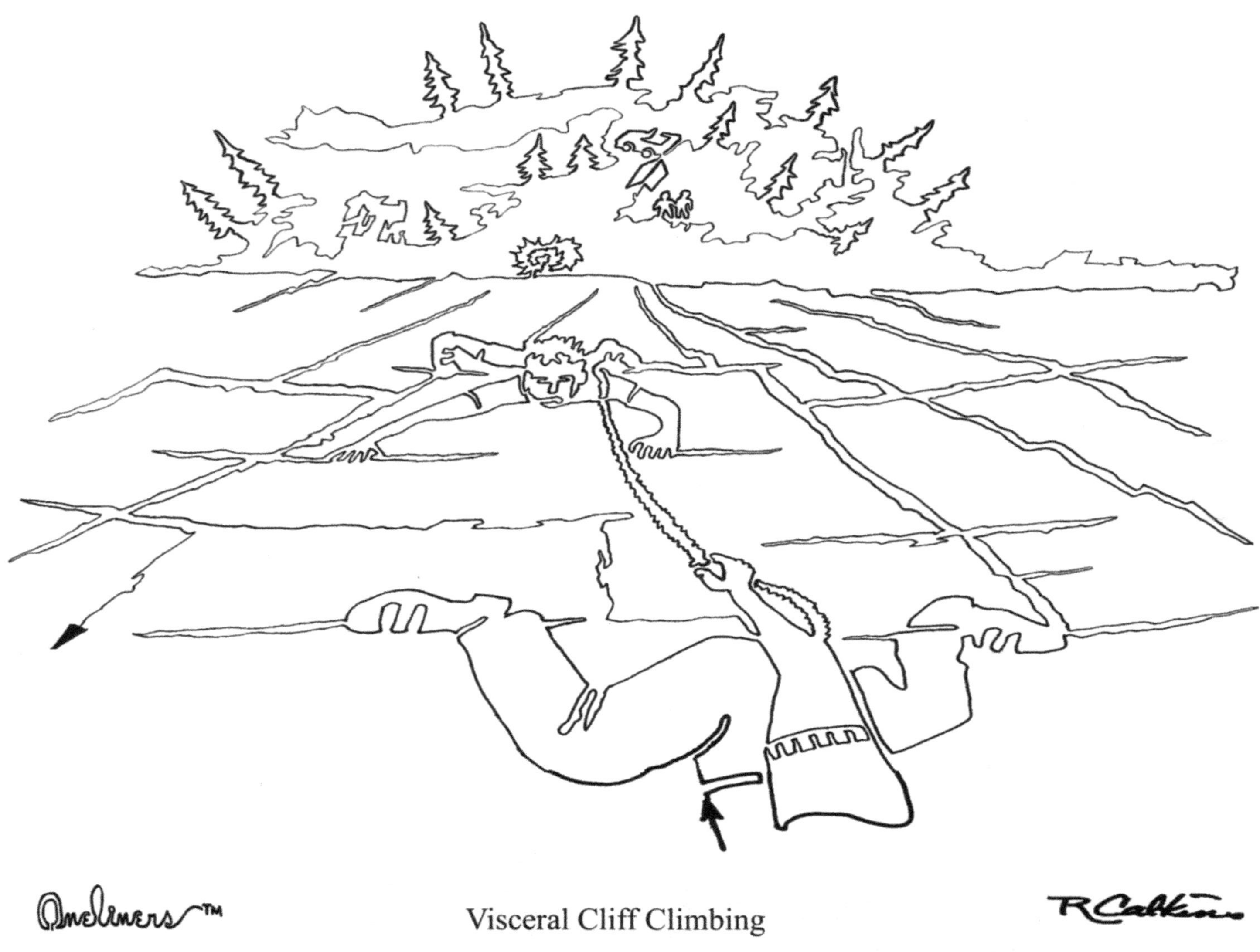

Visceral Cliff Climbing

Eye of the Predator

What immediately grabs your attention in this drawing?

For a little atmospheric background, let's say you're sitting on the bank of a some slowly moving water, known as a bayou in the American South. It's stiflingly hot and so humid you're sopping wet. The gazillion or so surrounding insects are deafening.

When you look up from baiting your fishing line you find yourself looking into the eye of the predator! He slowly exhales the breath he has been holding while he waits, completely motionless, for you to be distracted while he contemplates what to do about you . . . or to you. If he decides you're lunch, you won't even see him move. There'll just be an explosion of water, scales, and teeth.

Study everything that causes your response. Examine that baleful eye from the perspective of what we've learned about instinctive responses to line characteristics and to objects we see.

The line is thicker where it shows the predator's iris. This attracts your attention and tells you it's important.

The iris lines are vertical -- serious, imposing, unyielding, intimidating.

Your subconscious asks your instinct program what it thinks about the shape of the iris. It isn't big and round like a baby's or man's best friend. The xenophobia subroutine cries out "alien!" and the fight or flight instinct subroutine cries "run like the dickens!"

No wonder the first place you look is at the eye and that it gives you a shiver.

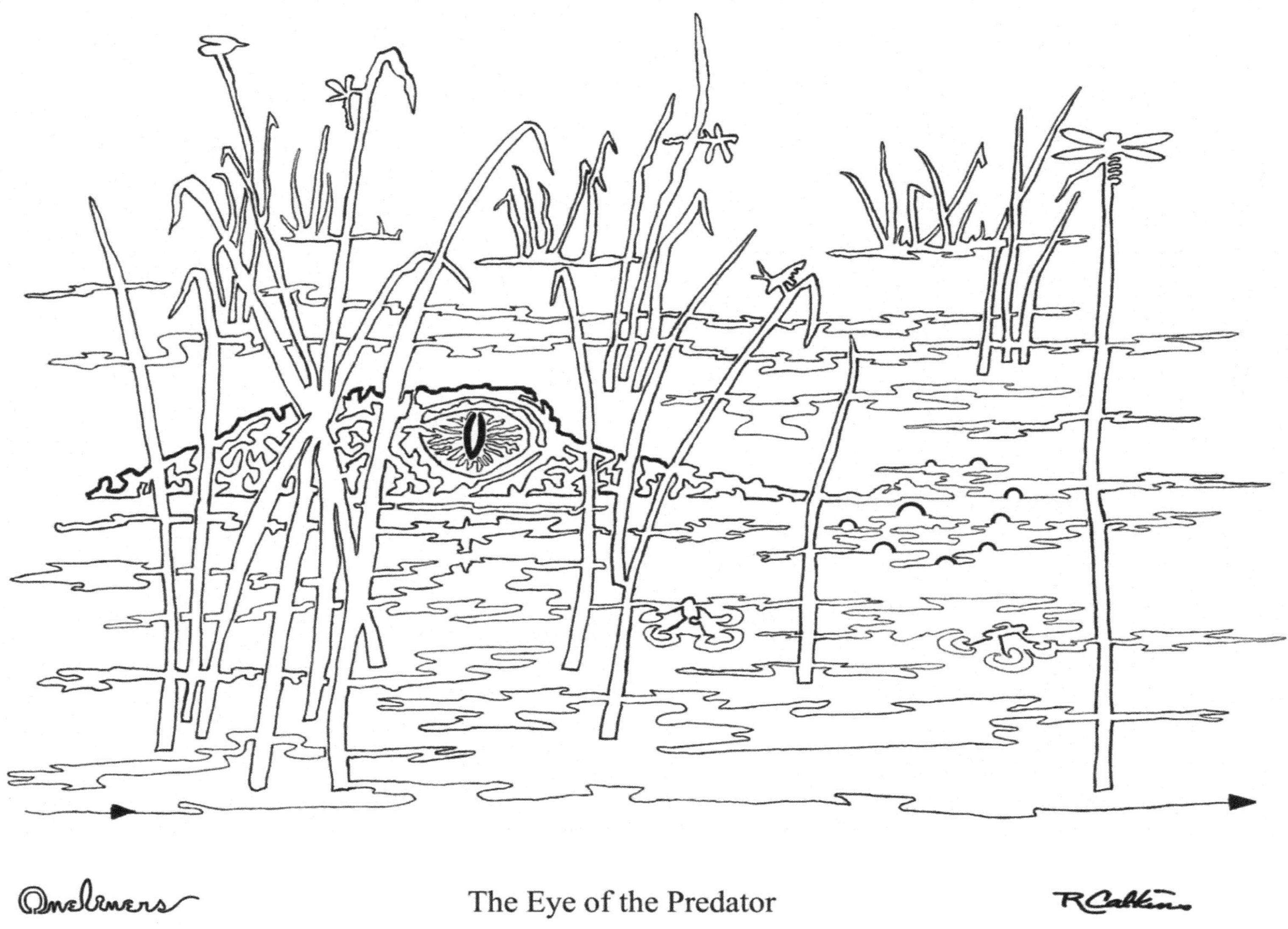

The Eye of the Predator

A Day at Mount Rainier

It's a brisk sunny day at Mount Rainier in Washington State. There's a wonderful scent of fir and cedar on the breeze and we can hear the cries of birds overhead. The scenery is just beautiful. There's even some wildlife to take pictures of. Now, if those noisy jets would just take some other route flying out of the Seattle-Tacoma airport.

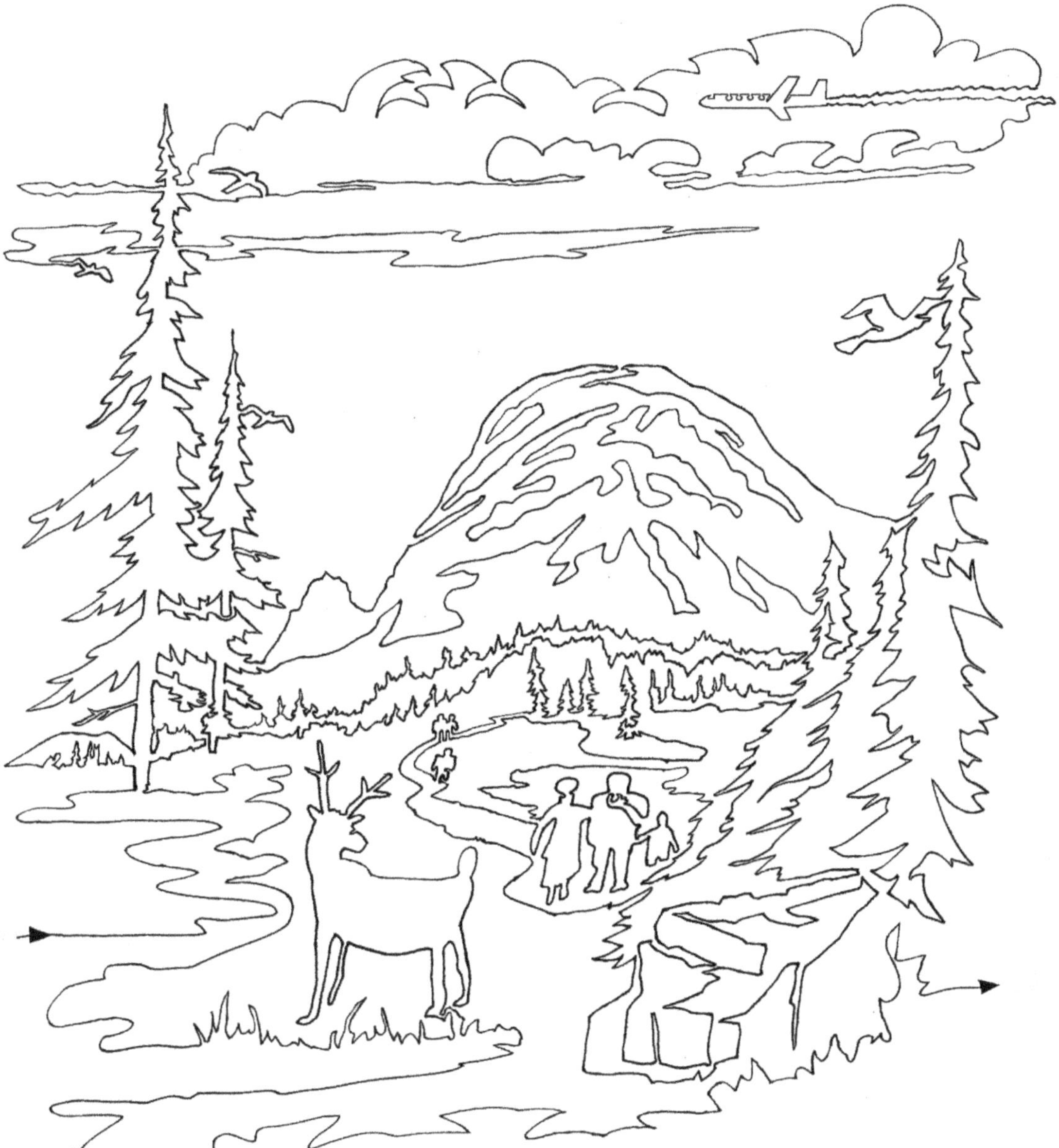

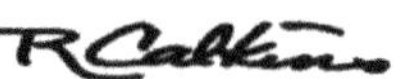

A Day at Mount Rainier

Castles by the Sea

Talking about brisk air, the mountains don't have anything over the Oregon coast. Even on a sunny day, the breeze coming off the ocean can be cold. There are people on the beach dressed for this weather in coats and hats. Some of them are admiring a man-made castle and others are admiring one built by a higher authority. The locals call these big rock formations haystacks.

Can you hear the cries of gulls and the surf pounding on the rocks? What are the things (objects or line characteristics) that tell you there is a stiff breeze blowing and that it's cold?

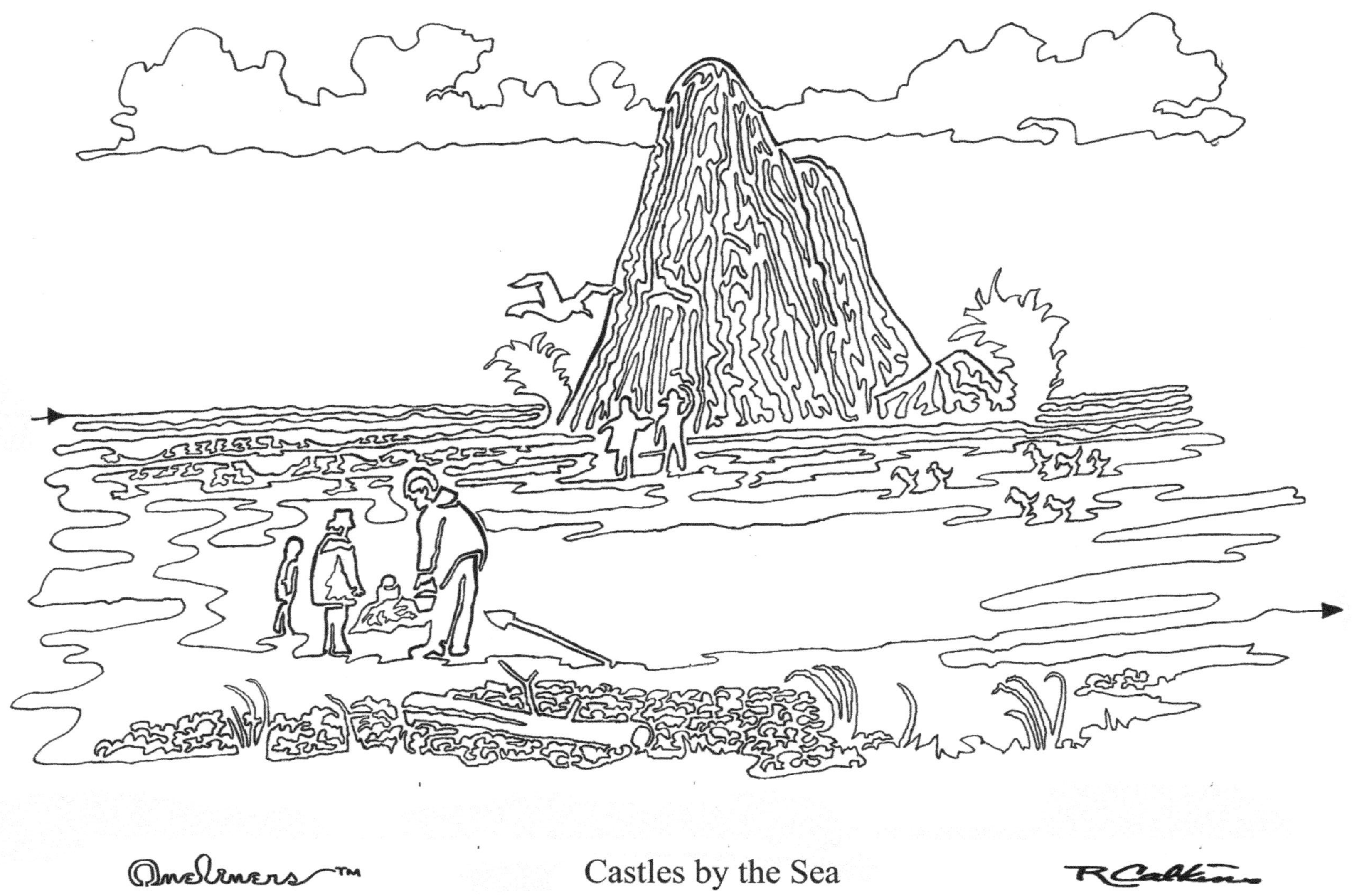

Castles by the Sea

Whales in Space

The line can exert such power that with a few strokes of the pen we can put whales in outer space. Here are mama and baby whale swimming gracefully through a sea of interstellar clouds. Perhaps they are on their way to visit Pisces.

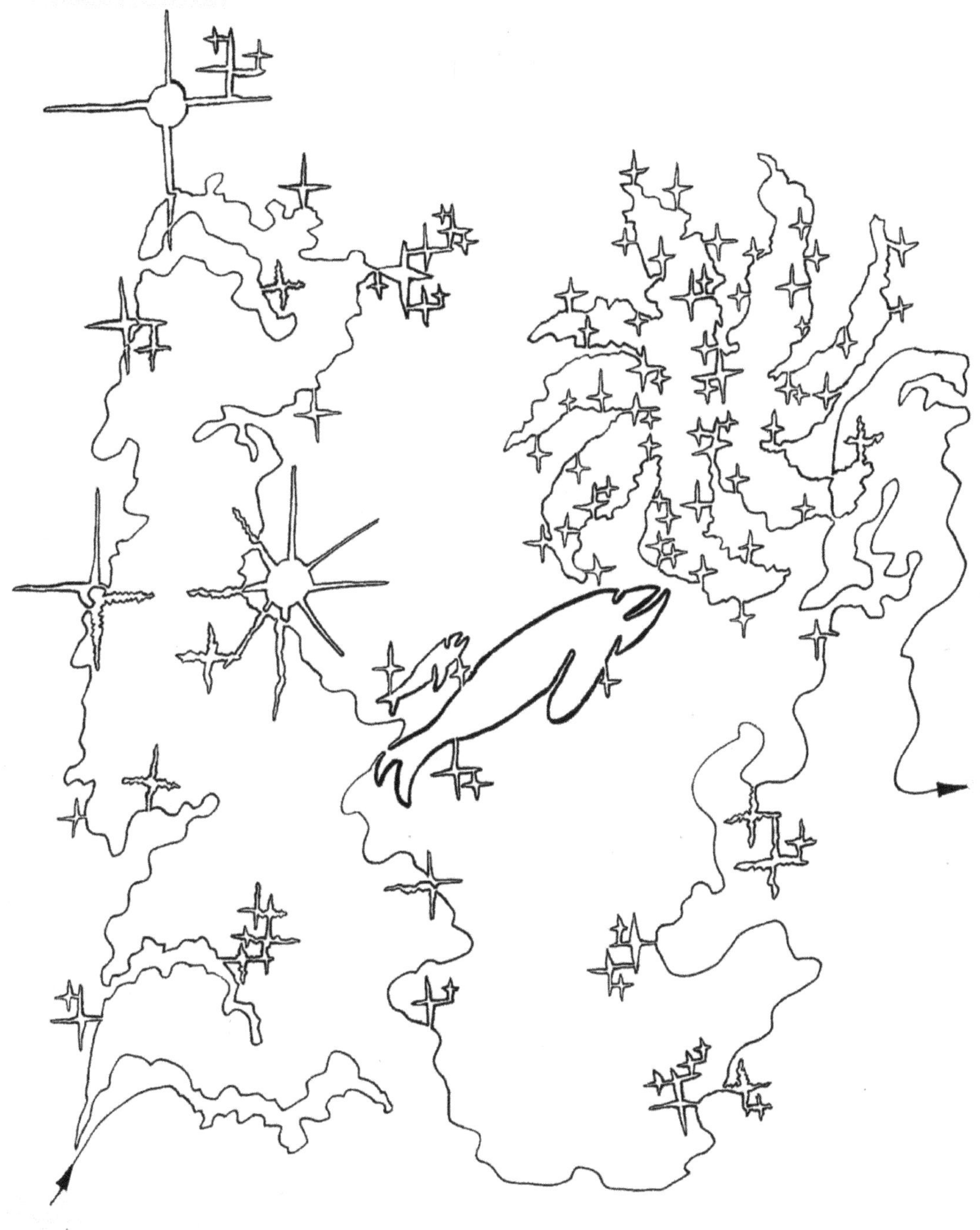

Oneliners ™
Whales in Space
R Calkins

Chapter 6
Summary

In keeping with the mission of A Different Perception, the purpose of this book is to give you a new perception of how a line can communicate. In the opening of this book I said you were about to become a magician by learning how to conjure and control the power of the line. Since every drawing in this book consists of nothing more than a single unbroken line, it is axiomatic that everything you've seen in them and your responses to what you've seen came from the power of the line. That single uninterrupted line is the only thing that's there.

You learned how the line can make you see things that cause you to respond emotionally. You saw how the characteristics of the line itself can be manipulated to have a similar effect. You also learned how the two can be used together to emphasize the result. You learned how to arrange groups of objects and their line characteristics to tell a story. You learned how to examine the causes of your response, which will facilitate your own study and experimentation into the power of the line. That's a lot of power delivered in one easy-to-read book.

Even if you've never picked up a pencil, you now have the knowledge of an Apprentice Magician of the Line. To become a Journeyman, you have only to put in some disciplined practice (which means doing a lot of drawing while you think about what you're trying to do, how you intend to do it, and how well you are succeeding). You already know a lot about your tools, how they work, and how to assess the results.

When you become a Journeyman, the universe is yours. You can choose almost anything you can see or imagine, make others see it through your eyes, and share at least some of what you feel about it. You don't have to use Oneliners; that was simply a tool to assure you that I didn't have anything up my sleeves. Oneliners can be useful, however, for a number of reasons: practice deciding what to put in and what to leave out, trying different compositions, or just plain fun trying to see how much you can do with a single unbroken line.

Becoming a Master of the Line takes a lot more time and discipline. It also takes a lot of self-teaching through experimentation and analysis. As you move into the realm of the Master, there are few out ahead who can teach you and you will develop your own unique and different style of how to make a line communicate.

At the beginning of our journey, I mentioned two myths to be banished: "I don't have to do drawings in order to paint" and "I can't do this because I can't even draw a straight line." The first has to do with how well you want to capture the essence of your subject, convey what you feel about it, and communicate your message. One of the battles we artists constantly wage, and often lose, is beautifully expressed in the old saw: "He put so much detail in the foreground that the background went underground." What we almost instinctively do when that happens is restore balance by putting so much detail in the background that the message goes underground. Drawing a few Oneliners of your proposed composition imposes a discipline that automatically helps you control that tendency.

One of the reasons we so often lose the battle with detail is because there is an almost irresistible urge to put in as much as possible "because it is there." After all, we think leaving out something that's there might make our drawing or painting look incomplete. But it simply isn't possible to paint every leaf, every twig, every branch, every bug, every spot of sun in the dappled sunlight -- well, you get the idea. If we leave all the decisions of what to put in and what to leave out until we're already painting, we're going to find ourselves studiously adding as much detail as possible to the background. (Trust me, it isn't pretty.) Doing a few Oneliners of your subject helps you win the detail war simply because you instantly come face-to-face with the need to choose what to leave out in order to get to what you really, really want to put in.

What's important is to decide what you want to say about your subject. Then examine it carefully to see what is the minimum amount of detail required to say it. Everything else belongs out of the picture unless there is a message-related reason to put it in (as discussed in the section Using Details Purposefully on page 26). Making good choices of what to leave out (or merely suggest without the clutter of detail) will put you way ahead of a lot of artists who have been at it longer than you have.

While the saying "I can't even draw a straight line" is put forth as a joke, the underlying message of "I can't make the pen or brush do what I want it to" is not a joke. It discourages a lot of people from becoming the artists they could be. What new artists need to know is that none of us can control the pen or brush with the accuracy we'd like. Control comes only with practice and never fully to our satisfaction. As any successful artist will tell you, being an exceptional artist requires acceptance of constantly falling short of your own expectations. That is because your expectations will grow as your knowledge and experience grow. If you truly want to become an exceptional artist, learn to accept falling short of your own expectations. That is the spur which leads to continuing growth. When you arrive at the point where you are fully satisfied with your abilities, you will cease to grow.

But also be aware that the really good pictures come from making the right choices about what to leave out, what to put in, where to put it, and what to do with its characteristics to deliver the message. Look at the paintings by the old masters. It is not unusual to see lines and brush strokes that we'd be less than happy with in our own work. How well you handle the pen or the brush will improve with practice, but that isn't what will make you a master. The better you learn to hone your decision process, the better your work will be, even if your technique never arrives where you are fully satisfied.

Now we're down to the last of the inducements I held out to you when you picked up this book. That is learning how to capture the universe on a single unbroken line. You've already learned how to create and chain Oneliners. We could readily chain every Oneliner in this book into one humungous line (with Mona Lisa at one end of it since she is not continuously chainable). If we all draw more Oneliners and add them to the line, it will capture more and more of the universe. All it takes to finish the job is commitment and a whole lot of time.

Have fun!

    Dick Calkins

A DIFFERENT PERCEPTION

If you liked *Oneliners*, you'll love
Adages and Aphorisms from Philosophilus

This fun to read book is the perfect adornment for your coffee table. It is guaranteed to catch the attention of guests, make them laugh, and stimulate conversation. It also is a great gift for your favorite curmudgeon. It presents the musings of a curmudgeonly philosopher in ancient Athens named Philosophilus. Philosophilus reportedly is being channeled by someone named Richard Calkins, who lives in the wooded hamlet of Sammamish in the wild realms of the Pacific Northwest. Here is a sample of Philosophilus' musings.

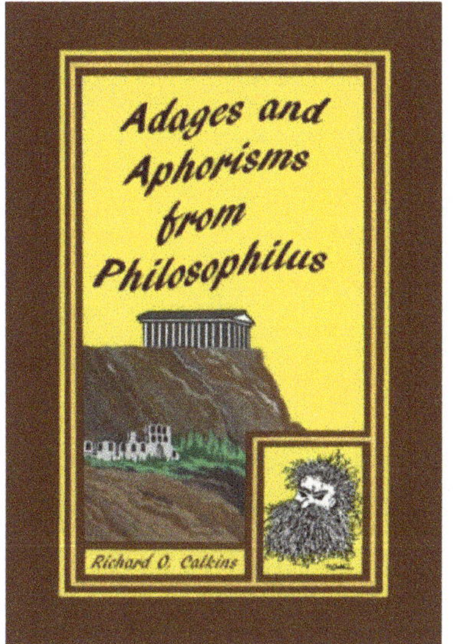

Over the vast panorama of history, human nature has proven to be remarkably resistant to change. This can be deeply distressing when dwelt upon.

Philosophilus

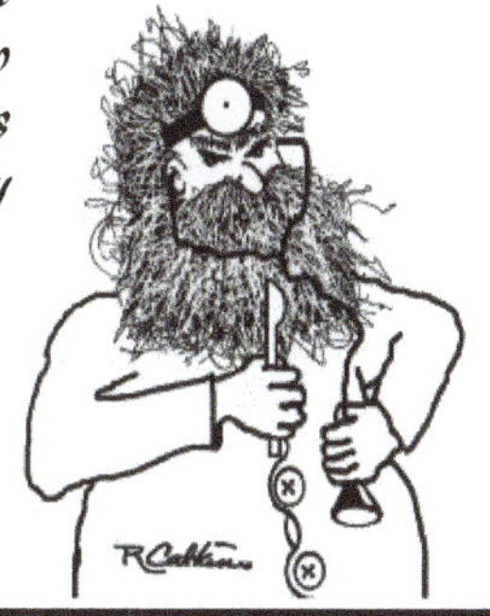

Physicians are highly trained practitioners of the healing arts who have learned to read the subtle nuances of our immensely complex human body to diagnose that which ails us.

Sometimes they are right..

Philosophilus

A diplomat is one who can deliver a mortal insult without offending its recipient.

A canny monarch knows better than to send a diplomat to deliver a well-deserved insult to a fellow tyrant. However, should your monarch be seeking someone to perform that service, anyone who is adequate to the task should take care to be occupied elsewhere.

Philosophilus

If you have a mind of your own, get used to being out of step and unpopular.

Philosophilus

Liberals and conservatives no longer listen to each other, and with good reason. Each already knows what the other is going to say and knows it to be wrong.

Philosophilus

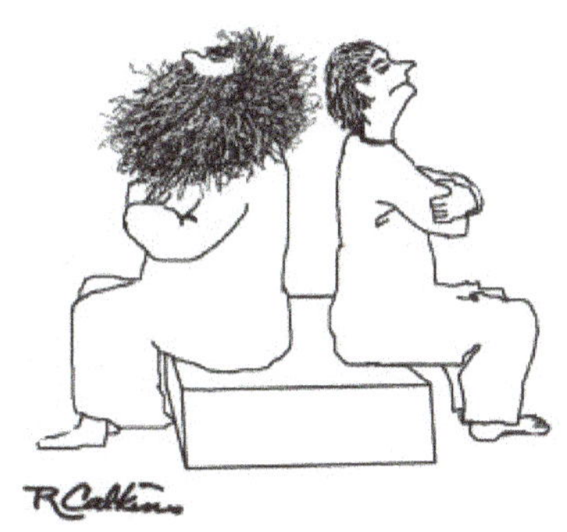

You can find *Adages and Aphorisms from Philosophilus* at Amazon.com and other online retailers.

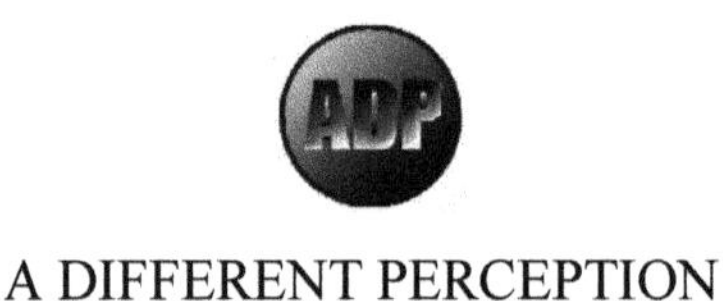

ADP
A DIFFERENT PERCEPTION

About the Author

Richard O. Calkins worked in the telephone industry for more than 40 years. Early in his career, he was a transmission engineer and later an Engineering Manager for network planning at Pacific Northwest Bell in Seattle, Washington.

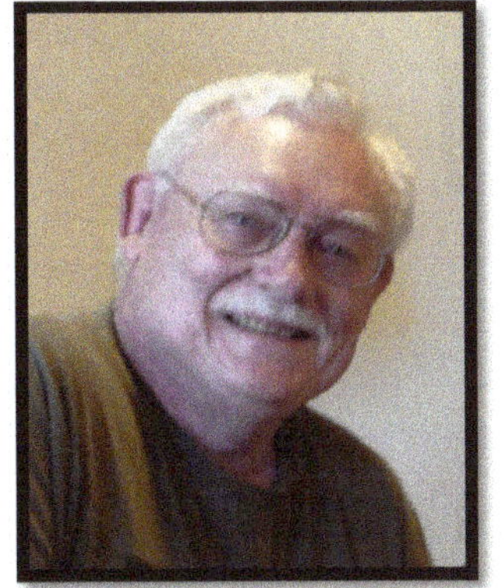

Following a move to GTE, he served in that company's Telephone Operations Headquarters in Stamford, Connecticut, where he held positions as Assistant Vice President for regulatory strategy and Assistant Vice President for product planning and pricing.

After retiring from GTE, he spent six years as Vice President for industry policy development at the United States Telephone Association in Washington, D.C. Since 1996, he has been retired in Sammamish, Washington, where he pursues personal interests in art, philosophy, and physics.

During his telephone industry career, Mr. Calkins was listed in Who's Who of American Business Leaders Special Edition, the Platinum Edition of the Who's Who Registry, and the Who's Who Registry of Global Business Leaders.

About Calkins Publishing Company

The mission of Calkins Publishing Company is to offer new and different perceptions of the things we take for granted. Our purpose is to introduce new insights on such subjects as art, science, philosophy, government, and the human condition. It is not incidental that our trade name is A Different Perception.

It is part of the human condition that everything we know is hostage to our assumptions. Some of our assumptions are explicit. We have the opportunity to assess their validity and to correct them as needed. Others are implicit; they are buried deeply in our subconscious where they tend to remain both unknown and unexamined. Yet they have a profound effect on how we think and what we believe. To open our minds and broaden our horizons, we occasionally need to excavate all of our assumptions and give them a good dose of sunlight and fresh air. It also wouldn't hurt to shake them up a bit with a good swift kick. Our goal is to provide points of view which will stimulate that excavation and reexamination. It also is to make you laugh and think while you're at it.

Please feel free to drop in on our website at www.calkinspublishing.com. You may be interested in some of the information provided there as well as in some of the free downloads. Questions may be directed to info@calkinspublishing.com.